# ROVER R8

T0294067

## JAMES TAYLOR

AMBERLEY

First published 2020

Amberley Publishing
The Hill, Stroud,
Gloucestershire, GL5 4EP

www.amberley-books.com

ISBN  978 1 3981 0121 0 (print)
ISBN  978 1 3981 0122 7 (ebook)

British Library Cataloguing in Publication Data.
A catalogue record for this book is available from the British Library.

Typeset in 10pt on 13pt Celeste.
Typesetting by SJmagic DESIGN SERVICES, India.
Printed in the UK.

# Contents

# CHAPTER 1

# The Background

In the first half of the 1990s, the Rover 200 and 400 models seemed to be everywhere. The 200 series was the strongest selling Rover of the period, and these medium-sized saloons were enormously popular as family transport, selling strongly to fleet users as well. The range was a wide one and included niche models that added interest and a little glamour.

On the whole, the R8 models (as their makers knew them) were dependable and solid cars. They played a large part in the revival of the Rover Group, which had sunk to an all-time low in the 1970s under its previous identity as British Leyland. A strategic alliance with Honda in Japan at the end of that decade had been a life saver, and the R8 was designed and built as part of that alliance.

The 200 and 400 were by no means traditional Rovers. The old Rover Company, which had been absorbed into British Leyland in 1968, had specialised in rather grander cars at the top end of the market. Through nearly twenty years of evolution, British Leyland had chosen the Rover name to reflect its intention of producing cars that were a cut above

The R8 range was made available as a hatchback 200 Series, with either three or five doors, and as a notchback 400 Series with four doors. These examples are 1994 model cars.

the average, and on the whole the ploy worked because the Rover name was still fondly remembered – and respected – in Britain. In terms of their market positioning, however, the R8s occupied a place that once belonged to companies such as Austin, and perhaps Riley.

Sadly, the fortunes of the Rover Group declined. Bought out by BMW in 1994, the company rapidly demonstrated that it could not meet the high-quality standards that its new German owners expected of it. By 1999 the Germans' patience had worn thin, and the company staved off its losses by selling the highly profitable Land Rover division to Ford. The cars side of the business was sold for a nominal sum to a group of venture capitalists; was renamed MG Rover; and collapsed in 2005. The Rover name lost whatever respect it had still retained, and by the time of the infamous scrappage scheme in 2009/2010, many owners were only too happy to weigh-in elderly 200s and 400s for a handsome allowance on a new car. Relatively small numbers survived, and it was really the low-volume niche models – especially the 200 Coupé – that kick-started enthusiast interest in the R8 range. Since then, it has grown steadily, to the point where a book like this is needed.

## Background

Throughout the 1980s, Rover (under its various names) was working closely with the Japanese company Honda on development of new models. The Rover R8 series came out of a fully collaborative project that involved engineers from both countries working to a common end. This was to deliver a design that could provide Rover with the basis of a new medium-sized car range, while also giving Honda a medium-sized saloon that would improve its sales in Europe. The result was extremely successful: Rover learned very valuable lessons about product development from the Japanese, and Honda learned a great deal about European market requirements from their British opposite numbers.

At first sight, the Rover R8 range appears hugely complicated, and to make its story easier to understand, this book breaks it down into major types. However, an initial overview – and the Timeline on page 8 – will probably help to make the picture clearer still.

Rover developed five-door hatchback and four-door saloon models in conjunction with Honda, who wanted these two models for their own Concerto range. However, the deal was that Rover could develop the basic designs in whatever way they saw fit once the joint designs had reached the market.

The five-door model was the first Rover announced and arrived in October 1989 as the 200 Series. The four-door Rover appeared a year later as the Rover 400 Series and was accompanied by a Rover-developed 200-series three-door variant that provided cheaper entry level models, as well as more sporting variants. These three variants remained the core of the Rover range right through until production ended in 1995.

Meanwhile, Rover developed the R8 range even further, beginning with a Cabriolet based on the three-door model and introduced in 1992. A few months after this came a Coupé based on the three-door platform but with unique body panels; both of these were named as variants of the 200-series. Then in March 1994 came the final major derivative, which was an estate car badged as a Rover 400 Tourer. These three derivatives, of which there were no Honda equivalents, remained in production after manufacture of the three core variants had ended, and their assembly did not end until summer 1998.

*Above*: All the first cars were 200-series five-doors, and a group is seen here at Lucknam Park in Wiltshire, the scene of the press launch.

*Left*: In October 2019, the Rover 200 & 400 Owners' Club recreated the Lucknam Park launch, thirty years after the event. This is a selection of the cars that attended.

This range of major derivatives came with a variety of engines, although not every derivative was made available with every engine. In the beginning, there were 1.4-litre K-series engines from Rover, and 1.6-litre engines from Honda. Over the years, there were several variants of the 1.4-litre engine, and the original SOHC Honda engine was joined by a DOHC variant.

In early 1991, two Peugeot diesel engines became available; one naturally aspirated and the other turbocharged. A 2.0-litre Rover engine was added later that year, and a turbocharged variant of it a year later. Meanwhile, Rover had been developing 1.6-litre and 1.8-litre K-series engines, and for the three derivative models – the Cabriolet, Coupé and Tourer – these replaced both the Honda 1.6-litre and the Rover 2.0-litre engines during 1996, although in practice the 1.8-litre size was unavailable in the R8 models until 1997.

The Cabriolet, Coupé and Tourer were R8 derivatives that were not shared by Honda. They remained in production after the mainstream models had been replaced. This picture shows the 1996 range.

## Siblings

Rover had introduced a new system of naming for its cars in 1984. At this stage, the company was strictly known as Austin Rover. The new system was inspired by the clear and readily understood BMW system, in which the series number denoted the size and status of the model and was followed by a pair of digits indicating the engine size. In the

This was the car that the first 200 Series models replaced. Also called the 200 Series, it was based on the Honda Ballade.

first half of the 1980s, there were 3-series compact models, 5-series medium-sized models and 7-series luxury models; a 318 was a 3-series with a 1.8-litre engine, a 518 was a 5-series with the same engine, and a 730 was a 7-series with a 3.0-litre engine.

The first Rovers named under the new system were the SD3 saloons introduced in 1984, which were known as the 200 Series and came as 213 and 216 types. The 200 name was deliberately chosen to position these cars one step below the BMW 3-series. Next came the 800 Series, which replaced the SD1 as the big-car range in 1986; there would be a 400-series derivative of the R8 range from 1990, and from 1993 there was a Rover 600 as well.

## R8 Timeline

| | |
|---|---|
| 1989, October: | 200-series launched as five-door hatchback saloon with 1.4-litre K-series or 1.6-litre Honda SOHC engines. |
| 1990, April: | 400-series launched as four-door notchback saloon with 1.4-litre K-series, 1.6-litre Honda SOHC and 1.6-litre Honda DOHC engines. |
| 1990, September: | 200-series three-door models introduced, with 1.4-litre carburettor and 1.4-litre injected K-series engines, or 1.6-litre Honda SOHC and 1.6-litre Honda DOHC engines. |
| 1991, March: | Diesel models added to 200 five-door and 400 ranges; 1.8-litre turbocharged engine and 1.9-litre naturally aspirated type, both built by Peugeot. |
| 1991, June: | 220GTi three-door model introduced, with 2.0-litre M16 engine. |
| 1991, November: | 400 range loses grey contrast panels and becomes available with 2.0-litre M16 engine. |
| 1992, April: | 200-series Cabriolet available, with 1.4-litre K-series and 1.6-litre SOHC Honda engines. |
| 1992, October: | Rover grille added to 400-series models; longer front indicator lenses for all models; multi-point injection for all 1.4-litre engines; T16 engine replaces M16 type; catalytic converters standard on all models; turbocharged T16 engine introduced for 220GTi Turbo and 420GSi Sport Turbo; Coupé introduced with 1.6-litre Honda SOHC (DOHC for export), 2.0-litre T16 and 2.0-litre turbocharged T16 engines. |
| 1993, November: | Rover grille added to 200-series models. |
| 1994, March: | Driver's airbag and belt pre-tensioners standard on all models. 400 Tourer introduced with 1.6-litre Honda SOHC, 1.8-litre turbocharged diesel, and 2.0-litre T16 engines. |
| 1995, early: | Last three-door 200-series and 400-series saloons built. |
| 1995, summer: | Last five-door 200-series built. |
| 1996, March: | 1.6-litre K-series and 1.8-litre VVC K-series engines replace 1.6-litre Honda and 2.0-litre T16 engines; R3-type dashboard for Cabriolets, Coupés and Tourers; 200 and 400 designations dropped for Cabriolets, Coupés and Tourers. |
| 1998, July: | Last Cabriolets, Coupés and Tourers built. Total production, 1989–1998: 953,699 cars |

# CHAPTER 2

# Developing the R8

By the time design work started in late 1984 on the car that would become the Rover R8, its manufacturers were approaching the sixth year of their co-operation with Honda. The first Honda-Rover co-operation had been a very one-sided affair, because the British company was in desperate need of a new medium-sized saloon to hold the fort until the new family of Maestro and Montego were ready in 1983 and 1984, respectively. So, the 1981 Triumph Acclaim was neither more nor less than a Honda Ballade built in Britain and re-badged.

The second collaboration with Honda produced the original Rover 200 range, known internally as the SD3 and in production from 1984. By the time Rover showed an interest in Honda's proposed new Ballade, the Japanese company had already done most of the groundwork, and so the British input to the new car was somewhat limited. The new Rover nevertheless had a Honda engine in its 213 guise and a Rover engine in its 216 guise, anticipating an engine-sharing strategy that would be continued later.

The third collaboration was far more ambitious, and in theory involved full engineering collaboration between the two companies to produce the 1986 Rover 800 and the Honda Legend. In practice this was less successful as a joint venture than the two companies had hoped, mainly because they had each worked independently on a core design. The results were a great deal of animosity and two cars that shared no more than about 20 per cent of their components – far less than was ideal and far less than had originally been intended.

So, when Austin Rover and Honda agreed in late 1984 to collaborate on a fourth new model, they already knew that they would need a more pragmatic approach. They decided that the best solution was to have a joint engineering team, and that when the thinking of the two companies diverged on an issue, they would adopt a single solution rather than different ones to suit each partner. It involved swallowing some pride on both sides, but the result was a project that ran very smoothly and delivered cars that shared an impressive 80 per cent of their components.

Austin Rover's requirement was for a car to replace the original Rover 200 series, which was a fairly conventional medium-sized four-door saloon with front-wheel drive. Honda's primary aim was to produce a car that was better suited to European tastes than their previous efforts, so that they could expand their presence in Europe. In the beginning, the two cars were known as the HY (the Honda version) and the YY (the Austin Rover version), but before long the British company changed its project code to AR8, the initials being an obvious reflection of its own name. When Austin Rover ceased to exist

The Rover R8 was designed by an integrated team of engineers from Rover and Honda, known as the Joint Engineering Team. In the centre, at the desk and facing the camera, is Ryuichi Takemura, Honda's resident chassis engineering representative in the UK.

in 1986 and the Rover Group came into being, the project code changed again to its definitive form of R8. The Japanese meanwhile chose a new name for their car, settling on Honda Concerto.

Much of the basic design work was done during 1985, and there was a great deal of British input during this phase of the project. Honda recognised that the Austin Rover designers and engineers had a far better grasp of European market requirements than they did and, as a key aim was for their new car to be successful in Europe, they tended to defer to the ideas that the British put forward.

Once the basic design principles had been agreed, Honda took the lead in engineering. Most of the engineering was actually done in Japan, by joint engineering teams that were made up of Honda engineers and British engineers, around twenty or thirty of whom went to live in Japan for the duration of the project. Those British engineers who have spoken of their experiences have said that the Japanese engineers were very friendly and that their engineering abilities were impressive; the Rover people learned a lot from them. From the outset, it was agreed that the British versions of the car would have both Honda and Rover engines, and the R8 was designed to accommodate both types. The Japanese models, however, would all have Honda engines.

## Styling

It is fashionable nowadays to refer to design rather than styling, but the older word was still common when the shape of the R8 and Concerto was being drawn up. Honda wanted a five-door hatchback as a basic model because they believed that would sell strongly on the European continent. Rover needed their car to replace the four-door 200-series saloons but came around to the Japanese way of thinking, partly because they saw scope for R8 to replace the hatchback Austin Maestro, which was then relatively new but had not dated well. Besides, once the basic design had been developed, the agreement between the two companies left each one free to develop additional models as it saw fit.

The Austin Rover styling department was based at Canley, where it had been headed since 1982 by Roy Axe. Both Honda and the British team put forward early proposals, and by all accounts these were quite similar. However, Honda allowed the British team to take the lead, again because of their greater experience of the European market, so Honda's preference for deep windows and shallow sides gave way to Austin Rover's preference for the opposite.

The chosen design had a slight wedge shape to it, although no special attention was paid to aerodynamics, and in fact the production models' Cd of 0.35 was not noteworthy for the time. Axe's preference for the understated look that he had used on the Rover 800 was carried over, although the R8 was a smaller car and needed more rounded shapes to give it the necessary presence. The grille and headlamp designs were carried over from the Rover 800, and the car was made to look sleeker than it really was by blacking-out all the window pillars to give a 'floating roof' effect. This was again carried over from the Rover 800, but the original influence may well have come from elsewhere: the Range Rover had benefited from the same treatment after mid-1981. A further distinctive feature was that the lower body sides were to be greyed out on cars of all colours, lining up with the tops of the bumpers and helping to slim the side elevation of the car.

The Japanese again stood back and allowed Axe's team to take the lead on the interior design, recognising that British interiors (on luxury models, at least) had a style and class that were the envy of manufacturers around the world. There was undoubtedly an important influence in the later stages of the design from Graham Day's desire to move the Rover brand more up-market, but there were carry overs as well. The driving position and the seats were very much in the mould of the Rover 800, while the overall design of the dashboard, with its low-set parcels shelf and prominent instrument binnacle, harked back to the one that Austin Rover had designed for the original 200 Series cars. Nevertheless, the instrumentation and switchgear were designed by Honda, whose expertise in these areas was acknowledged.

## Suspension

Suspension design was another area where Honda allowed Austin Rover to take the lead, although they kept their own counsel for Japanese versions of the car, insisting that they knew best what customers in the Asia-Pacific markets wanted. As a result, Japanese and European versions of the Concerto would have different floorpans.

All versions of the R8 and the Concerto would share the same rear suspension, which depended on the double wishbones that Honda favoured. It was at the front where the two companies' philosophies diverged. Honda wanted double wishbones again, but the

*Above left*: The front suspension used struts, which saved space and allowed maximum width in the engine bay.

*Above right*: This was the rear suspension, with the dampers inside the coil springs for compactness.

Austin-Rover preference was for MacPherson struts. These gave longer suspension travel and took up less space, so allowing for later changes at the front end if they became necessary. They were also cheaper than the double-wishbone set-up, so the R8 would always have them, and so would those versions of the Honda Concerto destined for European markets.

## Petrol Engines

Although Honda planned a variety of engines with 1.4-litre, 1.5-litre and 1.6-litre sizes, the Rover plan was simpler. The British company wanted just two sizes and was happy for Honda to supply its D-series engines to meet the requirement for a 1.6-litre; this would come in both SOHC and DOHC versions. However, from the start it intended to use its own advanced new K-series engine for the smaller capacity. This was eventually settled as a 1.4-litre size, for reasons explained below.

Development of the Rover K-series engines had begun in 1983, a year or so before the R8 programme had come into being. After a series of studies had demonstrated that further improvement of the existing A+ engine (which had started life under BMC as the A-series) would not meet the company's long-term needs, Austin Rover decided to develop a completely new one. Its chairman, Harold Musgrove, then had to argue long and hard to get approval for the development programme from the British Government, which owned the company at the time; the politicians' view was that a Honda engine could do the job perfectly well, and would save around £250 million in funding as well.

Like the A-series, the K-series engines were to be small-capacity types, and in the early days Rover experimented with a three-cylinder 1.0-litre size, which might have gone into a production version of the company's ECV3 concept car. However, the company abandoned this through fears of a negative public reaction, focussing instead on a 1.3-litre four-cylinder.

 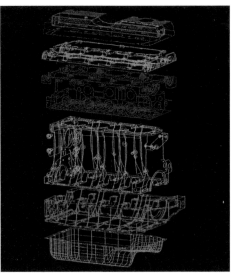

*Above left*: The R8 was the first model to use the new Rover K-series engine, of which the company was justifiably proud. This is a cutaway of the 1.4-litre version.

*Above right*: The revolutionary 'sandwich' construction of the K-series is clear from this computer-generated image. The multiple layers were held together by long bolts running from top to bottom.

This is the 1.4-litre K-series in place in a demonstration cutaway model that appeared at some early motor shows. The K-series was offset to the left of the engine bay; the Honda D-series was offset to the right.

Development progressed through the middle of the 1980s, and some of it was sub-contracted to Tickford at Milton Keynes, who had set themselves up as an engineering consultancy after separating from Aston Martin. Eventually, the Rover engineers settled on 1.1-litre and 1.4-litre four-cylinders, the latter because 1.4 litres had been proposed as one of the emissions certification boundaries. By ringing the changes with fuel systems (carburettors or fuel injection) and cylinder heads, they were able to achieve a wide variety of power outputs. One of the cylinder head designs had two valves per cylinder and a single overhead camshaft, while the other had four valves per cylinder and twin overhead camshafts; the two types had a high degree of interchangeability.

The four-valve (or K16) engine represented advanced thinking for a small family car engine at the time, but was the most effective way of minimising emissions while maximising power output, and, in a time before catalytic converters were the universal solution, Rover believed that clean-burn technology was necessary to meet ever-tightening emissions regulations. Both the SOHC and DOHC designs would have toothed belt camshaft drives, and the engines would be primarily intended for transverse installation in cars with front-wheel drive.

In the Advanced Engine Department, chief engineer Graham Atkin devised a radically new 'sandwich' construction for the K-series engine, which provided great stiffness while minimising weight. Some of its elements were derived from racing practice. Each engine consisted of four aluminium alloy castings located by dowels and held together by 16-inch-long bolts running from top to bottom. A conventional steel sump was bolted to the bottom.

The top casting functioned as a cam carrier and was a ladder-like item that contained the upper halves of the camshaft bearings. The lower halves of these were formed in the top of the cylinder head, which was the second casting down. Below that came the cylinder block, which formed the main casting and ended at the crankshaft centre line. Finally came the main bearing ladder, a deep-sided casting that contained the crankshaft bearings and also stiffened the bottom end of the engine. The design of the block, with its ladder frame, was a first in a mass-produced engine and gained Rover a good deal of respect when the K-series was announced after being refined and carried through to production under Sivert Hiljemark, Rover's Director of Powertrain Engineering.

By 1985 the ECV3 proposal had been side lined and Austin Rover were focussing on R8 as their new medium-sized car. The design of the K-series was frozen at the end of 1987; Validation build went ahead in 1988; and then in 1989 the Quality Proving and manufacturing-line batches were built. Although both 1.1-litre and 1.4-litre sizes were available, Rover's marketing chief, Kevin Morley, decided that the R8 should have only the larger size because that was consistent with the company's planned future as a premium manufacturer. A 1.1-litre model would have brought the entry point of the range down to a level that was just not consistent with that aspiration. The 1.4-litre engines for the R8 were tested in a fleet of 72 Montego 'mules'.

Like the K-series, Honda's D-series engines had been designed to meet a variety of needs by using different capacities, single or twin overhead camshafts, and carburettors or fuel injection. The first D-series engines were built in 1984, and over the years there were D12 (1.2-litre), D13 (1.3-litre), D14 (1.4-litre), D15 (1.5-litre), D16 (1.6-litre) and D17 (1.7-litre) base types. Rover chose the D16 engine in two different types, which were the D16A6, with a single overhead camshaft, and, for later introduction, the D16A8 with twin overhead camshafts.

These were all-alloy engines with cast-iron cylinder liners. They had a particularly neat ignition system that needed no HT lead, as both coil and transistorised ignition were built into the distributor, itself mounted on the end of the crankshaft. Like most Honda engines, they rotated in an anti-clockwise direction (as a result of the company's motorcycle origins), and so had to be installed differently from the Rover engines with their traditional clockwise rotation. In practice, the Rover engines were installed on the left of the engine bay while the Honda engines were installed on the right (in each case when standing looking into the engine bay).

## Diesel Engines

Like Honda, Rover intended to sell their new car on the European continent, but their perception was that it would sell most strongly in France, Portugal and Spain if it had a diesel engine. In the late 1980s, the only diesel engine in the Rover stable was the MDi or Prima 2-litre, which had been jointly developed with Perkins and was used in the Maestro and Montego family. This would have fitted into the R8, but its direct-injection combustion system was notoriously noisy, and Rover considered it was too unrefined for the job.

Rover had neither the time nor the funds to get a new diesel engine into production for the R8, and so the company took the decision to buy one in from another manufacturer. Their choice fell on the XUD range manufactured in France by PSA Peugeot-Citroën, which represented the state of the art in small diesel engine design at the time. As Rover's managing director, Kevin Morley, explained when the diesel engines were introduced in 1991, 'we have chosen this route in our quest for the most refined driving dynamics in the class. PSA is, of course, acknowledged as a leader in the installation of diesel engines in passenger cars. PSA's reputation will also help us develop sales on the continent.'

Diesel engines were planned, but were not in the initial release. This is the turbocharged Peugeot diesel that would become available during 1991.

15

The XUD was a range of small-capacity four-cylinder diesels suitable for transverse installation. When new in 1982, the engine was a big step forward for small diesels, with light weight, a high power output for the time and much greater refinement than earlier engines. Peugeot built several different sizes of this engine, but the ones that Rover chose were the turbocharged 1.8-litre XUD7TE and the naturally aspirated 1.9-litre XUD9A. Both engines had a single overhead camshaft and indirect injection, and were built at the PSA plant in Trémery, near Metz in north-eastern France.

The programme to develop the diesel versions of the R8 could not start in earnest until the basic engineering of the car had been signed off, and it was mainly for this reason that the diesel models would not be introduced until around eighteen months after the start of R8 production. In the meantime, Rover had also concluded a deal with PSA Peugeot-Citroën to build one of their gearboxes under licence for the R8 range.

## Gearboxes

None of the existing Rover gearboxes were really suitable for the new cars, and there were insufficient funds for Rover to develop a new one. So, the company did as it had been obliged to do for the Austin Maestro, and bought in those it needed from other manufacturers. For the Honda engines this was straightforward, as the Japanese company already had both manual and automatic gearboxes suitable for the job. The PG1 manual gearbox, designed by Honda but built by Rover, was also earmarked for use with the diesel engines. For the K-series engine, the problem was more difficult, and the engineers' choice eventually fell on the MA type that was made by PSA in France.

In this case, Rover did not use the gearboxes unaltered. The torque of the K-series engines was greater than that of the Citroën and Peugeot engines for which the PSA gearbox had been designed, and so Rover strengthened the casting, changed the bearings and fitted a larger differential. The British engineers also designed their own linkages and generally improved refinement, so that they were not unjustified in calling the finished article an R65 gearbox, the letter prefix suggesting that it was a Rover design.

## Ready for Launch

The engineering of R8 was completed in its essentials during 1987 and work now concentrated on last-minute fine-tuning of the design for its intended markets. Honda did theirs in Japan, and Rover did theirs back in Britain. They also began to think about the models that they could develop from the basic R8 package. Alongside the five-door hatchback that would be common to both companies, Rover wanted a sportier three-door hatchback and a four-door notchback saloon. Honda's focus was on that four-door saloon; they saw the five-door hatchback as secondary and had no interest in a three-door model because they already had their own entry in that sector of the market.

Meanwhile, Rover were investing heavily in new manufacturing facilities for the R8, the K-series engine, and the R65 gearbox. At a total cost of over £400 million, the new facilities were one of the largest investments in the company's history. Most of the money went into a new body plant, a new paint plant, and a new assembly track at the old Austin plant in Longbridge, where Rover would assemble not only their own cars but also Honda Concertos for European markets. However, £50 million of the total was spent to modernise and equip Rover's main pressings and tool manufacturing plant at Swindon.

16

The cutaway model shows how much was concealed behind that elegant dashboard.

The leather upholstery was an extra-cost option, but the shape and construction of the front seats are clearly visible here.

There was good room in the rear, too, as befitted a family car.

The whole manufacturing operation was fundamentally different from those that Rover had used before and was geared to allow each new car to be produced against a specific customer order.

During 1988, Rover also began to think about a series of low-volume niche models, and this period saw the first thoughts on Cabriolet, Coupé, and estate derivatives that would eventually see production in the early 1990s. There were thoughts about high-performance derivatives, too, using Rover's own powertrains, and about those diesel-engined models. None of these could be ready in time for the planned launch of the first R8 models in autumn 1989, but all of them would follow in the early years of the new decade.

An important question during the months leading up to the 1989 launch was what the new cars should be called. The five-door R8 would initially replace the existing Rover 213 and 216 models, and so it was only logical to bring it to market as the new Rover 200 Series. Under the BMW-style model numbering system explained in chapter 1, the names of 214 and 216 were automatic choices for the initial model release. Suffix letters could be used to indicate different levels of trim and equipment.

Looking further ahead, the plan was for the three-door models to be positioned slightly down-market of the five-doors, and for the four-door models to be positioned further up-market. The obvious-seeming choice of 100-series for the three-doors was not available because the existing Metro was to be renamed a Rover 100. So, the three-doors would have to be Rover 200s alongside the five-doors. As for the four-door saloons, the name of 400 series was an equally obvious choice. It avoided the use of numbers beginning with three (already claimed by both BMW and Volvo), and it left plenty of scope for larger models to be positioned below the existing Rover 800 at a later date.

Graham Day's plan to move the Rover brand more up-market had an effect at this stage. Rover were sufficiently confident of the appeal of the new R8 models to create a premium pricing structure, so marketing director Kevin Morley agreed a strategy of pricing the cars above their obvious direct competition. As a result, the entry level 214Si model was priced to compete with mid-range 1.6-litre cars from other manufacturers. It was an audacious move, but the market conditions were right: rival models had been around for several years and were showing it. Ford's Escort had been new in 1980, and the Volkswagen Golf and Vauxhall Astra had both been new in 1984. All were due for replacement shortly – but Rover had a golden opportunity to get the new 200 series established before its new rivals were introduced. It was a strategy that worked brilliantly.

# CHAPTER 3

# The Five-Door 200 (1989–1995)

Honda were quicker at getting their car on sale than Rover were, just as the Honda Legend had beaten the Rover 800 into production; the Japanese process of getting a car from design into production was far quicker than the British one. The Honda Concerto for the Japanese market was introduced on 15 June 1988, about sixteen months before the new Rover 200. Interestingly, Japanese customers were rather disappointed by the new car, although reactions would be quite different when the Concerto was launched into Europe.

The very first 'production' model was this 214GSi, which was equipped with a number of extras but, oddly, retained the standard wheels. It still survives, in enthusiast ownership. The grey-painted lower body panels were common to all the early cars.

*Above*: Proof of identity: this is the VIN plate of the first production car, with serial number 1. The plates on most production cars had entries in the panels for paint and trim, but this one did not.

*Left*: All the toys: the first production car had the options of air conditioning and leather upholstery, but its interior was otherwise visually to standard specification.

None of that affected the reception of the new 200-series models when they were introduced at the London Motorfair on 11 October 1989. The initial range of five-door hatchbacks consisted of four models, which were the 214Si, 214SLi and 214GSi, all with the 95PS 16-valve 1.4-litre K-series engine, and a 216GSi that had the 1.6-litre SOHC Honda engine with 114PS. Prices were indeed high, as planned, and the cheapest 214Si cost £8775, a figure that could easily be inflated by drawing on the options list. The top-model 216GSi cost £10,940 before options were added.

These first 200s were aimed at buyers with young families or young aspiring professional men and women. 'User choosers' – those able to choose their own company car – were also expected to account for a third of buyers, and private and small business buyers were a third category. The 200 was also expected to appeal to a proportion of older buyers, the sort of people who had helped to make the earlier 200-series Rover such a big success. An important part of the marketing programme at this stage was to stress the advanced technology of the cars, and to that end promotional literature regularly described them all as 16-valve types, and there was a small '16v' badge on every 200's tail panel.

The 200s followed Rover practice as seen on the 800 Sterling by having two-tone paintwork as standard, the bumpers and lower body sides being finished in Tempest Grey and contrasting with the main body colour. There were thirteen colours on offer, of which five were solids, seven were metallics, and one a pearlescent metallic. For the interior, Si and SLi models were trimmed in Zenith fabric, while the GSi models had Prism fabric. There were three colour choices, each assigned to certain exterior colours.

## What the Press Thought

British magazine *Autocar & Motor* latched on to the story of the R8 early on, and its issue of 30 August 1989 reported on a drive with the new 1.4-litre K-series engine in one of the Montego 'mules' that had been used for testing. First impressions were very favourable and would be confirmed when the magazine tested a 214Si a month or so later. First, though, they ran a comparison test between a Honda-engined 216 GSi and its rivals from Ford (the Escort Ghia), Renault (the 19 TXE) and Fiat (the 1.6 DGT SX). The results were published in the issue dated 11 October.

The cover headline said it all: the new 200 was 'good enough to beat the best'. The magazine described the 200 Series as 'a car for the aspiring young professional who demands style and driving pleasure in equal measure' and considered that the 216 GSi was 'a remarkably complete and well-executed car ... dynamically, it's spot on.'

The testers went on to say that, 'Rover's real achievement with the 216 has been to give it some class ... thoughtful detailing lifts it out of potential anonymity. The cabin is a minor triumph, too.' Although the car was priced between £1000 and £2000 above its most obvious rivals, 'it's worth the extra money: the quality shows.'

Like the 216 GSi provided for testing, the 214 GSi that *Autocar & Motor* tested for its issue of 1 November was a pilot-production car (and, amusingly, was registered with the licensing authorities as an Austin rather than a Rover). The magazine found the car to be 'a comfortable and fairly roomy four-seater but cabin width makes five a squeeze.' They thought that the 'high-speed ride quality is excellent, but the suspension is noticeably harsher at low speeds' and that there was 'no shortage of grip but body roll could be better controlled.'

The standard interior for both 214GSi and 216GSi was cloth, as seen here in a press picture released at the time of the launch.

Models were identified by neat badges on the tail. The 214Si was the entry level variant at launch time.

Slightly less plush than the GSi, perhaps, but the upholstery in this 214Si did give the appearance of quality and comfort.

The mid-range trim level was SLi. All models carried a small '16v' badge on the tail panel, as seen here.

The 1.4-litre K-series engine offered 'performance more than a match for many 1.6-litre engines' but it needed a sympathetic driver to get the best out of it. 'Performance is rarely found lacking in normal driving,' said *Autocar & Motor*, 'but a more languid driving style brings a reminder that this isn't a 1.6-litre engine after all; it must be kept spinning to achieve the desired results.' Of more concern, perhaps, was engine noise: 'mechanical resonance through the bulkhead is a constant companion' and 'a boomy mechanical presence is never fully isolated from the cabin and is often the most prevalent noise source.' On the positive side, however, the magazine had praise for the 'clean-changing' five-speed gearbox.

There were many other positive reviews in the press, and *What Car?* magazine gave the 214Si its coveted Car of the Year award for 1990.

## Expansion for 1991

Those first four models established a strong market presence for the 200-series models, and in September 1990 Rover followed up with a swathe of further R8 derivatives. There was one new five-door 200, together with the first three-door derivatives (see chapter 4) and the first 400-series four-door saloons (see chapter 5).

The new five-door 200 took over at the top of the range and also added a new sporting dimension to it. Called the 216GTi, it had the 130PS twin-cam version of the Honda engine allied to lower gearing for maximum accelerative ability; there was no automatic option. It was no doubt intended to attract younger buyers, and as evidence that this was in Rover's plan for 1991 the company also announced a range of body styling kits at the NEC Motor Show that opened on 18 September. There were kits for the five-door R8s and kits for the new three-door models as well, with prices starting from £725, but none of them proved very popular.

This rear view of a 1991-model 214GSi shows the discreet tail spoiler associated with the model.

The new models continued to come thick and fast. In January 1991 came a new 216SLi, with the same specification as the existing 214SLi but of course with the Honda engine. At the same time the 214S provided a new entry level model for the five-door range and became the first R8 derivative to have an SOHC eight-valve K-series engine, in this case with a carburettor instead of fuel injection; power output was 76PS. This model still had grey bumpers but did not have the matching grey paint below the rubbing-strip on its flanks. And then, just two months later, Rover introduced its diesel versions of the 200 range.

*Above*: The new top model for 1991 was the 216GTi, readily recognisable by its lattice-spoke alloy wheels. All early R8s had the maroon ('claret') highlights in the tops of the bumpers and in the side bump strips.

*Left*: The lattice-spoke wheels of the 216GTi were the earliest alloy wheel option on the R8 range.

The Honda engines rotated anti-clockwise, and so were differently located within the engine bay, with the 'front', or cambelt end, on the right in this picture of one in a 216GTi.

*Above left*: The 216GTi had a distinctive rear spoiler and, as this example shows, could also be bought with the option of a catalytic converter. Such things were new to Britain at the time and so their presence was advertised by another badge on the tail.

*Above right*: The 216GTi had Lightning cloth fabric upholstery with leather bolsters. This view of the rear seat makes clear that the cars had quite spacious passenger cabins.

The 'exclusive body styling' introduced in September 1990 is seen here with attractive alloy wheels (which were not then available) on a 214SLi model. Though in tune with the fashion of the time, the body kit did not sell very well.

Rover were very proud of the 'safety' steering wheel introduced on the 200 at its launch. Airbags would not be available until later.

## Adding Diesels

The diesel variants were the third swathe of new models in the 200 series. Rover knew that there was strong demand on the European continent for diesel power in saloon cars of this size, although British buyers were still rather diesel shy. However, diesel engines did not appeal to those who wanted a sporting element to their cars, and for that reason the bought-in Peugeot diesel engines would never be made available in three-door variants of the 200 series.

The new engines came with some constraints: there was no budget for alterations to the Peugeot specification. A particular problem was that these were quite tall engines, and when fitted under the standard R8 bonnet, their sumps hung down lower than the sumps on the Honda and Rover petrol engines. The Rover engineers solved that one by giving the diesel models longer springs, which increased the ride height by just enough to provide the clearance they needed under the sump.

The March 1991 introductions came as a 218SD, with a naturally aspirated 1.9-litre engine that gave 67PS, and a 218SLD Turbo, with a turbocharged 1.8-litre that gave 88PS. In both cases, the PG1 gearbox fitted the bill, although the two cars had different final drive gearing to suit the different characteristics of their engines.

The 218SD was conceived as an entry level model, and its trim and equipment levels mirrored those of the 214Si petrol model. There were, nevertheless, several features unique to the diesel model, which had an uprated 45Ah battery, a glow plug warning lamp, and a warning lamp for high coolant temperature or low coolant level. In addition, the greater weight of the diesel car called for a thicker front anti-roll bar and an additional anti-roll bar at the rear. The tyres had deeper sidewalls than on the petrol car, with a 175/70 x 14 size, and ventilated front discs were fitted as well.

The first diesel models were introduced in 1991. Badging apart, this 218SLD Turbo model was indistinguishable visually from the petrol-engined SLi models.

The 218SLD Turbo had all these features, plus power-assisted steering as standard. It also had a 'Turbo' badge on the rear appliqué panel. Trim and equipment levels otherwise mirrored those of the 214SLi model. The turbocharged diesel was considerably quicker than the 218SD, reaching 60 mph from rest in 11.8 seconds and having a maximum speed of 106 mph. The 218SD, by comparison, took 16 seconds exactly to reach 60 mph and was all-out at 96 mph.

## What the Press Thought

*Diesel Car* magazine tested a 218SD model for its June 1991 issue, and was impressed with the general air of quality and solid build. 'It feels a worthy successor to those solid Rovers of the 1950s and early '60s,' they said. The Peugeot engine was already well-proven in other cars and did its job well in the Rover. 'When worked hard it does start to sound definitely busy,' and its overall refinement was slightly disappointing; the 42.5 mpg achieved on test was also not quite as good as that of some competitors. Nevertheless, the 218SD was 'a good motorway cruiser, well able to maintain speeds up to about 90mph without strain, though inclines can call for a shift down to fourth.'

For just £250 more than the cost of the equivalent 214Si petrol saloon (at a time when diesels were invariably more expensive than petrol models), the Rover was good value for money. The magazine concluded that the car's 'particular virtues are clear. It's relaxing and easy to drive, it's comfortable and above all it exudes an air of quality at least the equal of a car like the Audi 80 ... if its general demeanour is a bit on the sober side, perhaps that's no bad thing ... the 218SD should ideally suit the growing ranks of diesel drivers who put a higher value on solid virtue than surface flash.'

## Holding Pattern: The 1993 Models

At motor show time in October 1992, the focus of activity within the 200 range was the introduction of the Tomcat Coupé, and the 200 Cabriolet was still relatively fresh, having been introduced only a few months earlier. Even so, there were several changes to the mainstream R8 models for 1993. Most visibly, the front indicator lenses were lengthened on all models – on the 400-series cars (see chapter 5) these were accompanied by a chrome grille. A slightly darker grey called Granite also replaced the flint grey interior trim. Less visibly, the entry level 214S three-door model disappeared (see chapter 4), and all the remaining 1.4-litre K-series engines switched from single-point to multi-point injection, putting power up to 103PS from the earlier 92PS.

For the moment, the new grille remained exclusive to the 400 range but, according to Rover publicity, the owners of existing R8s liked it so much that they began to ask for an appliqué version that they could fit to earlier models, so during the 1993 season Rover made one available. It was already obvious that the new grille would have to become standard, and its official introduction was in June 1993 on a special edition called the 214SEi.

The special edition consisted of both five-door and three-door models and was limited to a total of 7000 cars. Its purpose was to preview some new features and to strengthen the middle of the 200-series range. The five-door 214SEi could be had in just three colours and had steel wheels with 'prestige' trims (borrowed from the 400 range). Inside the cabin, it had sports front seats and Silverstone half-leather upholstery, with a burr

*Above*: This was the 214SEi Special Edition, which became available in summer 1994. It differed from the later line-built 214SEi in its grey bumpers and flank panels.

*Right*: Rover had taken care with the underbonnet appearance of their K-series engine. This is it in 1.4-litre 16-valve form, in one of the 1994 214SEi Special Edition cars.

walnut strip to enhance the facia. Electric front windows came as standard, along with a four-speaker radio-cassette installation, central locking, and a perimetric anti-theft alarm. As on other models below the SL level in the pecking order, a driver's airbag was an extra-cost option.

With the 1994 models scheduled for introduction in autumn 1993, Rover had always planned to make a number of changes that amounted to a mid-life facelift. To the specification already planned was now added the new chrome grille.

The November 1993 facelift brought with it a wholesale reorganisation of the range. A new entry level model was introduced as the 214i, once again with the eight-valve single-camshaft engine but now with injection instead of a carburettor, and with a 76PS power output. An entry level diesel model was introduced as the 218D and there was a new mid-range 218SD Turbo model as well, with the turbocharged engine.

There were changes to the model designations, too. Where the GSi name had once represented a luxury specification, it now indicated a sporty derivative and in effect replaced the GTi specification. One reason was that the GTi badge seemed to act like a magnet for joyriders, with the result that insurance costs for anything with those three letters on its tail had increased quite dramatically! The SLi specification was meanwhile realigned as the luxury trim level, so taking over from the old GSi.

The dependence on Honda engines was reduced as the 216GSi and 216GTi models were withdrawn, leaving only the 216SLi in production. Then the range was extended upwards with a new 220SLi that had the 136PS T16 engine already available in the three-door 220GTi (see chapter 4) and in the 400 series. It was positioned as a 'businessman's express' variant (and was known within Rover as the BMX).

The 1994 model facelift was spearheaded by standardisation of the new Rover grille. As this car shows, there were new wheel trims as well. The longer sidelamp lenses with curved trailing edges had been introduced a year earlier. This publicity photograph of an entry level model was described as a '214i/218SD/218SD Turbo'; it could have been any one of those models because they all looked the same!

Also new for 1994 was a 2-litre model. This is the 220SLi, with steel wheels wearing plastic wheel trims that give a convincing impression of the lattice-pattern alloys. That small 'power bulge' on the bonnet was shared with other 2-litre R8 derivatives.

From March 1994, a driver's airbag became standard equipment, bringing with it a new design of steering wheel. There were seat-belt pre-tensioners, too, which of course cannot be seen in this picture.

All this reshuffling was accompanied by some tangible differences across the five-door 200 range. The chrome radiator grille came with monochromatic light lenses, as introduced on the 400-series models a year earlier. While the entry level 214i and 218D models retained the old 'starfish' wheel trims, all other 200s with steel wheels now had full-diameter plastic wheel trims with a coloured Rover logo in the centre. All alloy wheels, on both petrol and diesel models, now had a seven-spoke design, and came with locking nuts as standard.

Side intrusion beams in the doors were now a standard fit, and so was remote central locking – except on the entry level 214i and 218D. So those models with central locking no longer had a keylock on the passenger's door, and at the same time all keys were changed for Z-slot types which were harder to copy than traditional keys. Then there were the inevitable changes to the paint options, and the grey upholstery option changed from Granite to the Ash Grey pioneered on the Coupés, although Stone Beige remained available as an alternative for some body colours.

From March 1994, there were further incremental changes, this time focussed on safety. All models now came with pre-tensioners for the front seat belts, and a driver's side airbag became available for the first time. Optional on lower-specification models, it was standard on the SL and above. Then from July, Rover made available a dealer-fit power-assisted steering conversion that could be added to earlier 1.4-litre models that did not have it.

## Pruning: The 1995 Models

The most obvious feature of the 1995 models that were introduced in autumn 1994 was that they now came with single-colour paintwork. The Tempest Grey lower contrast panels had gone, and the front bumper on all models was now what Rover called the sports style, with a large air inlet in the centre of the apron that was flanked by stylish brake ventilation slots. Rover probably believed that this fresh appearance would be an important aid to sales at a time when the new Rover 200 range was only a year away from its introduction.

The five-door range was very slightly pruned for this final model year, losing the top-model 220SLi (although some examples probably still lingered in showrooms for a few months). Still in production were the three 1.4-litre models (214i, 214Si and 214SLi), one 1.6-litre (the 216SLi), and the four diesels (218SD, 218SLD, 218SD Turbo and 218SLD Turbo).

A few further changes were held over until mid-December 1994, when a passive immobilisation system was added to the anti-theft measures, and the five-door 214Si and 218SD models gained interior wood veneer trim. At the same time, the 214SEi returned as a mid-range standard production model, with the same specification as the earlier limited edition of the same name but now with the single-colour paintwork and other 1995 model year changes.

The range was then gradually slimmed further, although (as before) older models doubtless lingered in the showrooms for some months to distort the picture. By April 1995, the 216SLi five-door model had gone, leaving just four 1.4-litre types (214i, 214Si, 214SEi and 214SLi) and four diesel types available. Production of the five-door 200 range then came to an end in summer 1995, and the cars were replaced in the autumn by the new Rover 200 series (known internally as the R3). The last 214 and 218 models provided showroom stock for Rover while production of the new R3 built up, but by Spring 1996 the vast majority had gone.

The 214SEi later became a standard production model, and an example of that displays the 1995 model and later features of single-tone paintwork and a redesigned front apron.

## Technical Specifications, Rover 200 five-door

*Engine*

1396cc K-series 8-valve with carburettor; 76PS (214S, 1990–1992).

1396cc K-series 8-valve with injection; 76PS (214i, 1993–1995).

1396cc K-series 16-valve with single-point injection; 95PS (214Si, 1989–1992; 214SLi, 1989–1992; and 214GSi, 1989–1992); Catalyst versions with 92PS.

1396cc K-series 16-valve with multi-point injection; 103PS (214Si, 214SEi and 214SLi, 1993–1995).

1590cc Honda D16A6 SOHC; 114PS (216GSi, 1989–1993; and 216SLi, 1991–1995).

1590cc Honda D16A8 DOHC; 130PS (216GTi).

1769cc Peugeot XUD7TE turbocharged diesel; 88PS (218SLD Turbo, 1991–1995; and 218SD Turbo, 1993–1995).

1905cc Peugeot XUD9A diesel; 67PS (218SD, 1991–1995; and 218D, 1993–1995).

1994cc M16 DOHC; 136PS (220SLi, 1993).

1994cc T16 DOHC; 136PS (220SLi, 1994).

*Gearbox*

Five-speed R65 (214) – Ratios: 3.417:1, 1.947:1, 1.333:1, 1.054:1, 0.854:1, reverse 3.583:1.

Five-speed Rover-Honda PG1 (all naturally aspirated diesels) – Ratios: 3.250:1, 1.894:1, 1.222:1, 0.935:1, 0.764:1, reverse 3.000:1.

Five-speed Rover-Honda PG1 (all turbodiesels) – Ratios 3.166:1, 1.842:1, 1.222:1, 0.848:1, 0.648:1, reverse 3.000:1.

Five-speed Rover-Honda PG1 (220) – Ratios 2.923:1, 1.750:1, 1.220:1, 0.935:1, 0.765:1, reverse 3.000:1.

Five-speed Honda PP7A-53 (216) – Ratios 3.250:1. 1.894:1, 1.259:1, 0.937:1, 0.771:1, reverse 3.153:1.

Five-speed Honda (216 GTi) – Ratios 3.250:1. 1.944:1, 1.346:1, 1.033:1, 0.848:1, reverse 3.153:1.

Four-speed Honda E4 automatic (216 auto) – Ratios 2.705:1. 1.560:1. 1.027:1, 0.780:1, reverse 1.954:1.

## Axle Ratio
3.937:1 (214, 218SD)
4.062:1 (218SLD Turbo)
4.200:1 (220)
4.214:1 (216 automatic)
4.250:1 (216 GTi)
4.437:1 (216)

## Suspension
Front independent suspension with MacPherson struts, forward facing tie bar and anti-roll bar. Rear independent suspension with double wishbones and compensating trailing arm; anti-roll bar on 216 and 218

## Steering
Manual or power-assisted Positive Centre Feel type.

## Brakes
214: 238 mm (9.4-in.) front discs and 203 mm (8.0-in.) rear drums.

216, 218 and 220 (and 214 with ABS option): 262 mm (10.3-in.) ventilated front discs and 239 mm (9.4-in.) solid rear discs. Bosch ABS 2E optional on 214, 218 and 220; Honda ALB2 on 216.

## Dimensions
| | |
|---|---|
| Overall length: | 4220 mm (166.2-in.). |
| Overall width: | 1940 mm (76.4-in.) over mirrors, 1680 mm (66.1-in.) excluding mirrors. |
| Overall height: | 1400 mm (55.1-in.). |
| Wheelbase: | 2550 mm (100.4-in.). |
| Track, front: | 1475 mm (58.1-in.). |
| Track, rear: | 1470 mm (57.8-in.). |

## Wheels and Tyres
214Si, 214SLi and 214GSi: 5J x 14 steel wheels (5.5J x 14 alloys optional), 175/65 x 14 TR radial tyres (185/60 x 14 optional).

216GSi: 5J x 14 steel wheels (5.5J x 14 alloys optional), 175/65 x 14 HR radial tyres (185/60 x 14 optional).

218 models and 220 models: 5J x 14 steel wheels (5.5J x 14 alloys optional), 175/70 x 14 radial tyres, HR rated on 220SLi.

## Kerb Weight

| | |
|---|---|
| 214Si: | 1030 kg (2271 lb). |
| 214SLi: | 1050 kg (2315 lb). |
| 214GSi: | 1065 kg (2348 lb). |
| 216GSi: | 1080 kg (2381 lb). |
| 216GSi (auto): | 1100 kg (2425 lb). |
| 216GTi: | 1120 kg (2470 lb). |
| 218D & 218SD: | 1140 kg (2515 lb). |
| 218SD Turbo & 218SLD Turbo: | 1185 kg (2610 lb). |
| 220SLi: | 1190 kg (2625 lb). |

## Performance

Max speed:

| | |
|---|---|
| 214: | 106 mph/105mph (with catalytic converter). |
| 216: | 120 mph/118 mph (automatic). |
| 216GTi: | 125 mph/122 mph (with catalytic converter). |
| 218: | 96 mph. |
| 218 Turbo: | 106 mph. |
| 220: | 125 mph. |

0–60 mph:

| | |
|---|---|
| 214 | 11.1 sec./11.5 sec. (with catalytic converter). |
| 216 | 9.2 sec./10.8 sec. (automatic). |
| 216GTi | 8.6 sec./8.9 sec. (with catalytic converter). |
| 218 | 16.0 sec. |
| 218 Turbo | 11.8 sec. |
| 220 | 8.2 sec. |

CHAPTER 4

# The Three-Door 200 (1990–1995)

Rover always treated the three-door variants of the 200 series quite differently from the five-door models, even though the only real differences between them lay in the bodyside pressings and associated interior trim. They even shared a tailgate. Designed by Rover without input from Honda, the three-doors were always intended to have a more sporting appeal than their five-door siblings. As a result, the engine line-up was often different between the two ranges, although there were also several model designations that were applied to both types.

The three-door models followed a year after the five-doors, and were announced in September 1990 at the NEC Motor Show. There were four derivatives at first, which started with a 214S that had the 76PS eight-valve carburettor engine and dispensed with the Tempest Grey lower body contrast panels. Next up was a mid-range 214Si with the

The entry level three-door model was the 214S, which did not have the grey lower contrast panels of other models. This early example has steel wheels with 'starfish' trims.

Representative of the mid-range three-door specification was the 214Si. The wedge shape of the lower body is very clear in this view.

The 216GTi came with the single-camshaft Honda engine. For the benefit of the press photograph, this one was dressed up with the new five-spoke alloy wheels that were standard on the Twin Cam cars but an extra-cost option on this model.

The overtly sporty variant was the 216GTi Twin Cam, which came with five-spoke alloy wheels, body-colour bumpers, no grey contrast panels, and the almost obligatory tail spoiler.

Clear in this picture of an early 216GTi Twin Cam are the twin exhaust outlets and the small 'Twin Cam' badge below the main model designation.

The body styling kit is seen here on the 216GTi Twin Cam. Most obvious are the larger boot lid spoiler and the twin openings in the rear apron.

16-valve engine, but above that were two overtly sporty models. The 216GTi came with the 116PS SOHC Honda engine, which delivered very respectable performance, and was readily distinguished from other models by a lip spoiler on the rear deck, like that on the 216GSi five-door. It had body-colour bumpers and lower body panels; the 214Si meanwhile had grey lower panels while the 214S had body-colour lower panels but grey bumpers.

At the top of this initial three-door range, however, the more expensive 216GTi Twin Cam had the DOHC version of the Honda engine, with 130PS and quicker acceleration than any other model in the 200 range. A small Twin Cam badge on the rear distinguished it from the single-cam GTi model (and, incidentally, was not on the five-door variant, which had the Twin Cam engine as standard). Twin bright tailpipes, 15-inch Roversport five-spoke alloy wheels and a larger rear spoiler were clear recognition features, and power-assisted steering was standard. Like the single-cam GTi, it came with body-colour bumpers and without the Tempest Grey lower body panels. It also came with a power-operated glass sunroof, and with upholstery that combined Lightning cloth with leather bolsters.

As on the five-door models, a Body Styling Kit was available as an option, and the new Roversport 15-inch alloy wheels could be ordered at extra cost for the models that did not have them.

## The Rover GTi Championship

Rover had a plan for promoting their new high-performance model from the start. With its introduction at the NEC Motor Show on 18 September 1990 came the announcement of a single-marque challenge for the 216GTi Twin Cam. A grid of thirty cars would contest the new championship, which was to be held at prestige venues throughout Britain, with one additional round on the European continent. The cars were to be developed under the supervision of former works driver Tony Pond, and were to have uprated suspension but standard engines. The standard glass sunroof would be deleted (for obvious safety reasons), and the cars would have a roll cage, racing seats and racing harnesses. Drivers would be sponsored by Rover dealers.

By the end of November, the details had been firmed up. Dunlop Tyres had become the lead sponsor, with Castrol and Delco in support, and the series would now be known as the Dunlop Rover GTi Championship. The cars themselves were to be delivered in the New Year and would cost £14,495 each – just over £300 more than a standard showroom model. There would be twelve races in the series, which would be administered by the British Racing Drivers' Club and would begin in April 1991. A thirteenth round would be held in France, at the charismatic Le Mans Bugatti circuit. The prize fund would amount to more than £100,000, and the winning driver would receive a 216 GTi Twin Cam as well.

This series provided some entertaining racing as support races during major motorsport events but was sadly marred by tragedy in June 1992. During the support race at the Coupe de Spa held at the Belgian Spa-Francorchamps circuit, driver Ian Taylor was killed in a multiple-car accident.

Some of the original race-series GTi cars have survived and are still campaigned in club racing events today.

The special race series for the GTi models in 1991/1992 had its own promotional sticker.

The GTi Championship cars were theoretically all to the same specification – so they were distinguished for the benefit of race goers by different paint schemes.

## What the Press Thought

The 216GTi Twin Cam went down well with *Motor Sport* magazine, which tested one for its April 1991 issue. There was particular praise for the gearbox, which was a 'perfect match for the high rpm engine, its close ratios engaged with a deft precision that makes one wonder if the complete arrangement is not electronic rather than metallic.' Overall, the Twin Cam had a most satisfying balance of driving qualities, which ensured that 'every non-motorway journey becomes an enjoyable prospect, every flowing country road a pleasurable outing.'

Like the five-door models of the 200 Series, the three-doors carried model identification on the tail.

*Above left*: R8s had high equipment levels. These electric windows are in a 216GTi.

*Above right*: Like other R8 models, the three-doors had the characteristic Honda style of radio aerial, which disappeared into the right-hand windscreen pillar.

However, not everything about the car came in for such high praise. The power-assisted steering 'proved accurate but said little to the driver about how the front Dunlops were faring under duress.' There was unwelcome engine noise at motorway speeds, and although 'the body does not noticeably suffer from the inevitable resonances of a four-cylinder power plant ... the small aluminium motor naturally sounds pretty busy about its motorway labours.'

Overall, though, the magazine thought this model would be a success. 'The combination of Rover's reviving reputation, the hidden charms of Honda and a brisk one-make racing series to glamorise the Rover product will ensure that the 216 GTi becomes one of those indefinable 'cars to be seen in.''

## Enter the 220GTi

Diesel engines were introduced for the five-door 200s and for the 400 saloons in March 1991, but Rover judged them inappropriate for the sporty three-doors, so there never would be any three-door diesels. Altogether more appropriate to the three-door range was the 220GTi model that was announced in June 1991. The 220GTi became the new flagship of the three-door 200 range, and as an additional selling point was made available with the option of pearlescent Caribbean Blue paint, which would not be available on any other 200-series models until later in the year.

The 220GTi was the first R8 model to have the 2-litre M16 engine, which would spread to the 400 range as well in the autumn. The engine had been introduced in 1986 with the Rover 800 saloons and was in effect a DOHC 16-valve derivative of the earlier O-series. Only ever available as a nominal 2-litre, its actual displacement was 1994cc from an 84.5 mm bore and an 89 mm stroke. In the 220GTi, it had multi-point injection (as in the Rover 820i) and developed 136PS at 6000 rpm, with 180Nm of torque at 4500 rpm.

Developed by the Rover Special Products division (see chapter 8), the 220GTi was a trailblazer for other high-performance R8 derivatives that were still under development. It was far and away the fastest car in the 200-series range at that time, with a top speed of

The 220GTi was a Rover Special Products confection. This press picture was issued in spring 1991 and shows the small bonnet bulge that distinguished these 2.0-litre cars, as well as the optional body-colour alloy wheels.

The 'Tony Pond spec' 220GTi was introduced in February 1992, and numbers were limited. The special front spoiler and vertically divided air intake are clear in this picture.

127 mph and a 0–60 mph time of 7.9 seconds. It was instantly recognisable, with a bodykit of sill finishers and spoiler that was painted in the body colour. Les immediately obvious was a small power bulge offset to the right of the bonnet, which was necessary to clear the camshaft drive of the M16 engine. Body-colour alloy wheels were an extra-cost option, and so was an ABS braking system. Otherwise, the specification was the same as that of the 216GTi Twin Cam, with the addition of a burr walnut facia insert.

On 25 February 1992, after the 220GTi had been on sale for around seven months, Rover announced a modified version with suspension that had been developed in collaboration with Tony Pond Racing; the suspension was stiffer and the car sat 20 mm lower than before, and the 'Tony Pond spec' cars were distinguished by a special divided air intake and a front spoiler that incorporated fog lights. These cars were available alongside the 'standard' 220GTi, but probably only 500 were built. The 220GTi continued in production for a further eighteen months but was replaced in the summer of 1993.

## Realignment for 1992

The arrival of the 220GTi was a clear signal that Rover intended to reduce its dependence on Honda engines and to rely instead on its own. Although the new model was briefly available alongside the 216GTi Twin Cam over the summer of 1991, the Honda-engined car disappeared from Rover catalogues in the autumn. So did the carburettor-engined 214S, which did not have the catalytic converter that was going to be required on all new cars sold in Britain after the end of 1992. This reduced the three-door range to three models, which were the 214Si, the (single-cam) 216GTi, and the 220GTi. It also left Rover without a 200-series car that cost under £10,000.

Further revisions were in the pipeline, and to help clear stocks there was a 216 Sprint special edition between October and December 1991; it was really a 216GTi but had steel wheels where the standard 216GTi would get lattice-spoke alloys from January 1992. Then Rover reintroduced a sub-£10,000 model in April 1992, respecifying the 214Si with a sports steering wheel, sports wheel trims, a front bib and a body-colour rear spoiler and dropping its price to £9,995 from the £10,940 previously asked. Bizarrely, a press release of the time described it as a 214i special edition model of which there were to be just 2,000 examples. Perhaps that was the original intention; this would not be the first time intention and reality had failed to agree!

## Going Turbo

The 1993 line-up of three-door models announced in autumn 1992 consisted of the same three models as before, stocks of the 214i special edition having been exhausted (at least, in theory). That meant there were 1993 model 214Si, 216GTi and 220GTi models available, all of them with catalytic converters as standard. Like their five-door counterparts, the 1.4-litre models now had multi-point injection and 103PS. The 220GTi, meanwhile, now switched to the new T16 engine.

Rover had also become rather nervous about price increases, and on 7 September announced what it called a 'new deal for Rover customers'. The announcement was wrapped up in some PR speak about removing doubt and uncertainty for potential buyers at a time when other manufacturers were using tactical discounting to attract customers, while increasing prices generally. In reality, what happened was that the company saved

The new entry-level 214i models had 'starfish' wheel trims and grey lower panels. Both three-door (foreground) and five-door variants were available from spring 1993.

costs by introducing a leaner distribution process, in which dealers no longer carried bulk stocks of cars, so list prices were reduced by up to 7 per cent. They went up again by an average of 2.9 per cent in December.

December also brought a new flagship model for the three-door range, increasing the total up to four again. The newcomer was called the 220GTi Turbo, and it used the same 200PS turbocharged T16 engine that had made its debut in the 220 Coupé Turbo at motor show time in October (see chapter 7). This enormous power in such a lightweight car gave a 0–60 mph acceleration time of 6.4 seconds and a maximum speed of 146 mph – not quite as fast as the 220 Coupé Turbo but still exciting for a medium-sized five-seater saloon car. Like the similarly engined Coupé model, the 220GTi Turbo relied on a torsen differential to prevent front-end traction problems and, as in the Coupé, the solution was only partially successful.

The 220GTi Turbo was always built in limited numbers and lasted in production only until the summer of 1993. As a result, it is now one of the rarest 200-series derivatives, although the absence of records means that no reliable production figures are available. Estimates of 250–500 are probably not far off the mark, and of these it appears that a good number were shipped to Japan. It does not look as if any examples were produced with left-hand drive.

There was one more special edition in February 1993, which was a 214 with the 'Sprint' badge that came in Caribbean Blue and had power steering as standard. Then, in parallel with the five-door models, the close of the 1993 model year brought a three-door 214SEi limited edition. Trim and equipment levels were exactly the same as for the five-door,

*Above*: The special-edition three-door 214SEi came with smart new wheel trims and the red bumper highlights associated with performance models.

*Left*: This was the attractive interior of the 214SEi three-door, with Silverstone trim.

although the three-doors were available in a more restricted range of just three colours, which were British Racing Green (metallic), Nightfire Red (pearlescent) and Tahiti Blue. The 214SEi name would of course return early in 1995.

### The 1994 Revisions

Like the five-door models, the three-doors were quite extensively revised for the 1994 model year. There were once again four models, but the line-up was new. Only the 214Si was carried over from the previous year, and the 214i was a new entry level model, taking on the name pioneered on the special edition cars during 1992. Above these then came two new names, which were 220GSi and 220GSi Turbo.

The production 214i was less exciting than the special edition had been and came with only 76PS from its eight-valve engine. Its cost was kept down by deleting

The revised range for 1994 included a 220GSi Turbo. The car came with the six-spoke alloy wheels seen in this press picture, although the absence of the small 'Turbo' badge from the tail suggests that this was actually a plain 220GSi dressed up for the occasion.

*Above left*: The genuine 220GSi Turbo had a badge to prove it.

*Above right*: Every self-respecting high-performance car had to have a tail spoiler in the 1990s, and this was the one on the 220GSi Turbo.

power-assisted steering, and of course it had drum brakes at the rear like the 214Si. There were 13-inch steel wheels with plastic 'starfish' trims and, again like the 214Si, it retained Tempest Grey lower body panels and black door mirror bodies. The price at launch in November 1993 was by far the lowest of any 200-series model, at £9180; a 214Si cost £10,325.

The 220GSi and 220GSi Turbo were really the old 220GTi and 220GTi Turbo under new names. The switch to a GS designation, which up to this time had indicated luxury top models, had been made for the same reason as it was on five-door models; to avoid heavy insurance premiums on anything with a GTi badge. In practice, they had lost none of their earlier performance qualities, and still retained the sporty-looking bodykit.

All the 1994-model three-doors had the chrome grille and monochromatic light lenses that became standard on the five-door models at the same time. The two GSi models had seven-spoke alloy wheels, and the 214Si had steel wheels with the new plastic trims that had a central coloured Viking ship emblem. All models, except the 214i, had remote central locking, no keylock on the passenger's door, and Z-slot keys. Paint options were revised, as for the five-door 200s.

Again, like the contemporary five-door 200s, the 1994 model three-doors all had side intrusion beams in the doors. The two GSi models gained a height-adjustable driver's seat, and Ash Grey interior trim took over from the lighter Granite type, while Stone Beige remained an option with some colours. March 1994 brought standard pre-tensioners for the front seat belts on all models and a driver's side airbag for the two GSi cars, although this was an extra-cost option for the 214i and 214Si. Earlier 1.4-litre three-doors without power-assisted steering could also have the new retro-fit conversion after July.

If the extra plumbing for the turbocharged T16 engine did not give the game away, there was no mistaking that 'Turbo' designation on the inlet cover.

*Above*: This is a non-turbo 220GSi with the seven-spoke alloy wheels that were standard on those cars. The coachline was not a standard feature.

*Right*: These stickers were available through Rover dealers when the cars were new.

The 214 Sprint name was revived in May 1994, this time not for a factory produced special edition but as a set of extras that dealers could add to three-door cars already in stock to aid sales. The extras were limited to a Sprint badge on the tail panel, and floor mats with a Sprint logo. The result was priced at £750 less than a standard 214Si, which made

it something of a bargain at the time. Rover's original plan seems to have been that the base cars were all to have metallic paint, but later examples (the promotion lasted until early 1995) certainly included cars with solid paint colours such as Flame Red, and quite possibly some 214i host models as well.

## 1995: The Run-Out Models

The four mainstream 1994 models remained available for the 1995 season that began in autumn 1994, so there were once again 214i, 214Si, 220GSi and 220GSi Turbo choices, all the 1995 cars being distinguished by single-colour paint and by sports-style bumpers with brake vents.

As was the case with the five-door models, the range was tweaked in mid-December 1994 when a passive immobilisation system was added and the 214SEi returned as a mainstream derivative. Unlike the mainstream five-door 214SEi, the three-door always had old-style Tempest Grey contrast panels together with old-style grey bumpers; perhaps Rover had found a stock of the unpainted bumpers and decided to use them up!

One way or another, there were probably relatively few examples of the three-door 214SEi because three-door production was wound down in the first quarter of the year to make way for the new R3 200 range that was to be released in the autumn for the 1996 model year. No doubt a quantity of three-doors remained in showrooms until and perhaps even beyond the summer of 1995, but they were not listed in documents issued to Rover staff after March 1995.

Rover used the Sprint name several times on special-edition models that were mainly intended to clear stocks. This one was clearly based on a 214Si and was sold new in the Netherlands.

# Technical Specifications, Rover 200 Three-Door

## Engine

1396cc K-series 8-valve with carburettor; 76PS (214S, 1990–1992).

1396cc K-series 8-valve with injection; 76PS (214i, 1993–1995).

1396cc K-series 16-valve with single-point injection; 95PS or 92PS with catalytic converter (to 1992).

1396cc K-series 16-valve with multi-point injection; 103PS (from 1992).

1590cc Honda SOHC; 114PS (216GSi, 1989–1993; 216GTi, 1990–1993, and 216SLi, 1991–1994).

1590cc Honda D16A8 DOHC; 130PS (216GTi Twin Cam).

1994cc M16 DOHC; 136PS (220GTi, 1993–1994).

1994cc T16 turbocharged DOHC; 200PS (220GTi Turbo, 1992–1993; 220GSi Turbo, 1993–1995).

## Gearbox

Five-speed R65 (214) – Ratios: 3.417:1, 1.947:1, 1.333:1, 1.054:1, 0.854:1, reverse 3.583:1.

Five-speed Honda PP7A-53 (216) – Ratios: 3.250:1. 1.894:1, 1.259:1, 0.937:1, 0.771:1, reverse 3.153:1.

Five-speed Honda (216 GTi) – Ratios: 3.250:1. 1.944:1, 1.346:1, 1.033:1, 0.848:1, reverse 3.153:1.

Five-speed Rover-Honda PG1 (220) – Ratios: 2.923:1, 1.750:1, 1.220:1, 0.935:1, 0.765:1, reverse 3.000:1.

Four-speed E4 automatic (216 auto) – Ratios: 2.705:1. 1.560:1. 1.027:1, 0.780:1, reverse 1.954:1.

## Axle ratio

3.937:1 (214).

4.200:1 (220).

4.214:1 (216 automatic).

4.250:1 (216 GTi).

4.437:1 (216).

## Suspension

Front independent suspension with MacPherson struts, forward facing tie bar and anti-roll bar. Rear independent suspension with double wishbones and compensating trailing arm; anti-roll bar on 216 and 220.

## Steering

Manual or power-assisted Positive Centre Feel type.

## Brakes

214: 238 mm (9.4-in.) front discs and 203 mm (8.0-in.) rear drums.

216 and 220 (and 214 with ABS option): 262 mm (10.3-in.) ventilated front discs and 239 mm (9.4-in.) solid rear discs. Bosch ABS 2E optional on 214 and 220; Honda ALB2 on 216.

## Dimensions

| | |
|---|---|
| Overall length: | 4220 mm (166.2-in.). |
| Overall width: | 1940 mm (76.4-in.) over mirrors/1680 mm (66.1-in.) excluding mirrors. |
| Overall height: | 1400 mm (55.1-in.). |
| Wheelbase: | 2550 mm (100.4-in.). |
| Track, front: | 1475 mm (58.1-in.). |
| Track, rear: | 1470 mm (57.8-in.). |

## Wheels and Tyres

214S and 214i: 5J x 13 steel wheels; 155SR13 (214S) or 155TR13 (214i) radial tyres.

214Si: 5J x 14 steel wheels (5.5J x 14 alloys optional), 175/65 x 14 TR radial tyres (185/60 x 14 optional).

216GSi: 5J x 14 steel wheels (5.5J x 14 alloys optional), 175/65 x 14 HR radial tyres (185/60 x 14 optional).

220 models: 5.5J x 15 alloy wheels, 185/55VR15 radial tyres (220GTi and 220GSi), 195/55ZR15 radial tyres (220GTi Turbo and 220GSi Turbo).

## Kerb Weight

| | |
|---|---|
| 214i | 1010 kg (2225 lb). |
| 214Si | 1020 kg (2250 lb). |
| 216GTi | 1095 kg (2415 lb). |
| 216GTi Twin Cam | 1110 kg (2450 lb). |
| 220GTi | 1195 kg (2635 lb). |
| 220GSi | 1175 kg (2590 lb). |
| 220GSi Turbo | 1190 kg (2625 lb). |

## Performance

Max speed:

| | |
|---|---|
| 214S | 101 mph. |
| 214Si | 113 mph. |
| 216GTi | 120 mph/118 mph (with catalytic converter). |
| 216GTi Twin Cam | 125 mph. |
| 220GTi | 127 mph. |
| 220GTi Turbo | 146 mph. |

0–60 mph:

| | |
|---|---|
| 214S | 12.5 sec. |
| 214Si | 10.1 sec. |
| 216GTi | 9.5 sec. |
| 216GTi Twin Cam | 8.6 sec. |
| 220GTi | 7.9 sec. |
| 220GTi Turbo | 6.4 sec. |

# CHAPTER 5

# The 400 Saloons (1990–1995)

Rover always saw the four-door saloon derivative of the R8 as appealing to a very different group of owners from those who would buy the two varieties of the 200 range. When the car was launched, on 28 March 1990, they described the customers as ranging 'from the up-and-coming executive, who wants style and exclusivity with a modern, dynamic image, to the driver who has been accustomed to large cars, but now wants a smaller vehicle with the least possible compromise in terms of elegance and prestige'. From the beginning, the 400 saloons were priced slightly above their five-door 200 equivalents. A 414Si, for example, cost £10,260 as against the £9990 asked for a 214Si, and a 416GTi was £14,995 while its 216GTi counterpart was £13,950.

The 400 models shared all their 'chassis' elements with the 200 and had the same 2550 mm (100.4-in.) wheelbase; engines and gearboxes were also common to the two

The distinctive rear-window style of the 400 was carried over from the Montego and worked very well. This is an early 414Si model, with the 'starfish' wheel trims and grey contrast panels.

ranges. The 400 shared the chiselled lines of the 200 range, but was different behind the rear doors, where Roy Axe had redesigned the rear of the cabin to resemble that of the Montego saloon. This provided a welcome family resemblance while giving the car a very clear identity of its own, and it was so successful that Honda adopted it for the three-box version of their Concerto that was developed from the same joint project. The capacious boot added a little to the overall length of the body, and the 400 was 145 mm (5.7 inches) longer overall than the 200.

The rear lamps and appliqué tail panel were carried over from the 200 range, but the rear bumper was unique to the 400. Inside the passenger cabin, most elements were also common to the two ranges, although the 400's rear seat had a fixed backrest rather than the split-folding type of the hatchback models. Interior trims and exterior colours were also shared with the 200 range, and the early 400 models all had the same Tempest Grey lower panels.

## The First 400s

There was a four-model line-up for the 400-series in the beginning, and the variants were badged as 414Si, 414SLi, 416GSi, and 416GTi. The two 414 models had the same 95PS 1.4-litre K-series engine as their equivalents in the 200 range and could be had in 92PS form with a catalytic converter at extra cost. The better-equipped 416GSi of course had the 116PS SOHC Honda engine, and the 416GTi became the first R8 derivative to have the 130PS twin cam Honda engine, as used in Honda's CRX Coupé. In the Rover, this delivered very respectable figures of 124 mph and 0–60mph in 8.6 seconds.

One step up from the 414Si was the 414SLi, distinguished most obviously by its different wheel trims. This is an early pre-production car; only a very few showroom cars gained G-prefix registration numbers.

This is another pre-production model, this time a Honda-engined 416GSi. Badges apart, there were no obvious visual differences from the smaller engined car with the GS specification.

There were thoughts of selling the 416GSi in Australia, and this one was dressed up with optional alloy wheels to gauge public reaction at a motor show there. However, Rover Australia were unable to price the car competitively and so decided against taking any.

Twin tailpipes, alloy wheels and, of course, a 416GTi badge; this was the top of the range model when the 400 was introduced in 1990.

However, the 416GTi was not just about performance, and Rover had specified it as a compact luxury saloon as well, with Positive Centre Feel power-assisted steering as standard, leather upholstery, electric windows on all four doors, and a top-notch ICE system. Several commentators have pointed out that the 416GTi was deliberately priced to rival German cars like the Audi 80 2.0E, BMW 318i and Mercedes-Benz 190E, and although in such company it was unfortunately rather out of its depth, the model nevertheless did have its own appeal.

Both varieties of 416 could be ordered with air conditioning and an automatic gearbox at extra cost. ABS was optional on all four 400 models, and there was a long list of other options. To simplify production, there were two option packs for the 416GSi; one combining power-assisted steering with the 185/60 x 14 tyres on 'lattice-spoke' alloy wheels used on the GTi, while the other combined power steering with leather upholstery and electric rear windows.

## What the Press Thought

Most magazines had already tried a 200-series model in recent memory, and so avoided devoting a full test to the new 400 because it was very obviously similar to it. However, *What Car?* tried a 414Si in its October 1990 issue, comparing it with a Renault Chamade, a Vauxhall Belmont, and a Ford Orion. The Rover, which was the most expensive of the four, was declared overall winner. 'It's an inspired car that exudes class and gives confidence – and prestige – to everyone who sits behind the wheel and drives it.'

The testers praised its 'sweet-running and turbine smooth engine', although they noted that on a motorway, 'slight inclines affect fifth gear cruising performance, and necessitate

The 416GTi won the Caravan Club's Towcar of the Year award for 1991.

The 416GTi of course had the twin cam Honda engine, with very clear 'DOHC' identification and 130PS when allied to a manual gearbox. In automatic form, it was slightly less powerful.

a downchange to maintain speed.' The Rover also just won the handling and ride category, with its 'sporting handling and smoothly damped ride'.

On the inside, 'the front seats are comfortable and well-bolstered,' but 'the rear seat is an uninspired bench.' Nevertheless, the '414Si exudes a 'quality' feel. Carpeting and seat materials are of a high order, and (despite the deletion of wood-veneer inserts on the 'base' car) it remains a thoroughly 'British' concoction.'

## Minor Adjustments: The 1991 Cars

The first 400s went down well, and Rover had no need to make any major adjustments at motor show time in the autumn, so the range was simply expanded to six models, with new 416Si and 416SLi types to strengthen its centre ground. Both had the 116PS SOHC Honda engine, and both could be had with an automatic gearbox at extra cost. Just as Rover had designed a bolt-on bodykit for the 200s, so they introduced one for the 400, with prices starting at £740 for the set of elements in primer.

Meanwhile, the 400 had started to attract awards, and in early November the Caravan Club announced that a 416GTi had won its Towcar of the Year title for 1991, as well as winning its class for cars priced between £12,001 and £17,000. The judges described it as 'a marvel of sheer all-round ability, the most complete car in its class', and added that 'the class beating flexibility of its power train is matched by a superb interior in the Rover tradition.'

From March 1991 there were diesel options, too. This was the 418GSD Turbo and displays appropriate badges on its tail. Note the small 'Turbo' identifier low down, next to the taillight.

### Diesel Models

The 400-series range got its diesel models at the same time as the 200-series, in March 1991. However, there was no entry level model for the more expensive 400, and both types had the 88PS turbocharged Peugeot engine. They were called the 418SLD Turbo and the 418GSD Turbo; the SLD Turbo had SLi levels of equipment, plus a Turbo badge on the tail, and the 418GSD Turbo was equivalent to a 416GSi. Both used the new PG1 gearbox that also appeared in the diesel-engined 200-series models, and there was no automatic option.

Both, of course, had unique features as well. Their diesel engines needed an uprated 45Ah battery, a glow plug warning lamp, and a warning lamp for high coolant temperature or low coolant level. Like the 200 diesels, they had longer springs to give ground clearance under the sump of the Peugeot engine. These were accompanied by a thicker front anti-roll bar and an additional anti-roll bar at the rear, 175/70 x 14 tyres and ventilated front brake discs. On the negative side, neither could be ordered with the air conditioning that was optional on petrol-engined models.

### The 1992 2-Litres

The 1992 model year brought yet more changes to the 400 range, and these were announced at the end of November. The two 1.4-litre models remained, the two turbodiesel models remained, and the two SOHC 1.6-litre models remained. However, the 416GTi disappeared and in its place came no fewer than four new models at the top of the range. These were badged as the 420SLi, 420GSi, 420GSi Executive, and 420GSi Sport, and all of them had the new 136PS Rover M16 2-litre engine, allied to the PG1 gearbox.

The M16 engine was still new to the R8 range, having made its bow a few months earlier in the 220GTi models (see chapter 4). Rover claimed that it delivered a maximum speed of 126 mph and a 0–60 mph acceleration time of 8.1 seconds in most 420 models, figures that somehow improved to 127 mph and 7.9 seconds for the 420GSi Sport.

The 420s all came with twin chrome tailpipe finishers, Positive Centre Feel PAS, uprated front and rear suspension and a thicker rear anti-roll bar. Trim and equipment levels of

*414Si/416Si wheel trims.*

*414SLi/416SLi/416GSi/418SLD/418GSD/420SLi/420GSi wheel trims.*

*420GSi Executive Prestige alloy wheels.*

*420GSi Sport 5 spoke alloy wheels.*

This was the range of standard wheels available for the 1992 model year. The early 'starfish' type had now gone.

The low angle helps to make the 1992-model 420GSi in this picture look more impressive than it really was, but the new Roversport five-spoke alloys played their part as well.

*Above*: As Rover saw it, the 420GSi Sport would appeal to the smart, young executive who was going places. This media release picture for the 1992 model-year makes the point.

*Left*: Lightning cloth with leather bolsters and fillets of traditional-looking Rover wood trim added to the sharp-suited image of the 420GSi Sport.

the 420SLi and basic 420GSi brought no surprises, but the other two models had features designed to appeal to the two extremes of the anticipated market, so the 420GSi Executive came with leather upholstery and steering wheel trim, 14-inch alloy road wheels, electric windows on all four doors and the top-specification stereo-radio cassette player of the time. Like the later five-door 220SLi model (see chapter 2), it was unofficially known within Rover as the BMX variant (for 'businessman's express'), and to give a softer ride it was fitted with the suspension from the diesel models, which had longer springs that had originally been designed to raise the ride height.

The 420GSi Sport, meanwhile, was clearly intended to replace the 416GTi in the range, so it came with half-leather sports seats in grey, 185/55 x 15 VR tyres on five-spoke alloy wheels, and 'sports' suspension (which actually meant standard springs that gave a ride which seemed sporty by comparison with that of the Executive model). There were body-coloured bumpers, front and rear spoilers, a black appliqué tail panel, rear wheel arch spats and rubbing strips with coloured inserts.

There were improvements right across the 400 range for 1992. The Tempest Grey lower panels now disappeared from all variants, and new bright finishers for the rubbing strips and bumpers replaced the earlier claret type. There were new wheel trims for the Si models. Five new paint colours were introduced, to join six carried over from the 1991 model year.

Interior changes were no less far-reaching. New front seats had originally been developed for the bigger 800-series cars, and there were new interior trim materials: Renaissance for the SL level, Chevron for the GS, Lightning with leather bolsters for the 420GSi Sport and of course full leather for the 420GSi Executive. Interior colours were now either Flint Grey or Stone Beige. The Si models now had burr walnut facia and door inserts, and ICE systems were upgraded across the range. And, in line with Rover's long-term plan to move the whole range gradually upwards in the market, there was a new luxury option pack for the 416GSi and 418GSD Turbo. This added leather upholstery and a leather-trimmed steering wheel, plus electric rear windows to match the standard electric front ones.

## New Grilles and New Models for 1993

The 400 range evolved again in October 1992 when the saloons became the first of the R8 models to take on a new front end that incorporated a chromed grille similar to that pioneered on the facelifted 800 models a year earlier. The new grille certainly added a more distinctive look and was perceived as adding 'class', and in this respect it helped to justify Rover's deliberately high prices for the 400 range. The original idea was for it to remain exclusive to the 400 derivatives of the R8 range, but it went down so well with customers that Rover decided to standardise it on the 200 models as well a year later. On the 400s, as indeed on the 200s later, the grille was accompanied by monochromatic rear light lenses.

However, that was not all, and the 1993 Rover 400 range boasted two new engines. One was a direct replacement for the M16 engine in the 420 models, and the other was a high-performance turbocharged version of this. The new engine was called the T16 and was a further development of the M16 that had been introduced for the facelifted Rover 800 models in autumn 1991. Rover policy was now to replace all M16-engined cars with the new engine.

The T16 engine shared its 16-valve DOHC configuration and its bore and stroke dimensions with the earlier M16. It came as standard with a catalytic converter and

The 1993 models came with the new corporate Rover grille and with longer lenses for the indicators. The wheel trims seen here deliberately resembled the earlier alloy wheel design. This is a diesel derivative, but from this angle it is impossible to tell for certain which one it is.

The 420GSi Executive was developed as a 'businessman's express' model, and brought a more sophisticated, less sporty demeanour to the car.

developed 136PS at 6000 rpm with 185Nm of torque at 2500 rpm. Yet despite the similarities, there was a great deal of difference between the old and the new engines. The T16 was tidier externally, the pipes of the M16 having been turned into internal channels. The cylinder head, cam profiles and pistons were all new, and the crankshaft had twice as many counterweights. The cam belt no longer drove the water pump, which shared an

For 1993, the 420GSi Sport Turbo brought serious performance to the 400-series range. The fog lights were a standard feature.

auxiliary drive belt with the PAS pump. The engine management was now a MEMS 1.3 system, designed for use with a catalytic converter, and a long-tract inlet system increased the ram-air effect to give much better torque, which peaked at 2500 rpm rather than the 4500 rpm of the earlier engine.

This, then, was the new engine for the 420SLi and 420GSi, and for the Executive and Sport derivatives of the latter model. Its turbocharged derivative was introduced in the new 220 Coupé Turbo at the same time, and although most of the publicity focussed on that car because it was the flagship of a new Rover range, the new 420GSi Sport Turbo came with exactly the same 200PS power output, and the same torsen differential that was intended to minimise traction problems.

There was just one more new model in October 1992, and this brought another engine that was new to the 400-series range. The new model was a 418SLD, with the non-turbocharged Peugeot diesel engine that was otherwise only available in the five-door 200-series cars. While it was not a major success, it undoubtedly sold more strongly than the limited availability 420GSi Sport Turbo and must also have brought in considerably more profit for its makers than that model ever did!

### 1994: A Reshuffled Range

The 400-series range was shuffled again in November 1993 for the 1994 model year. The 416GSi was dropped, although the 416Si and 416SLi remained available, and the SLi was upgraded to very nearly GSi specification. The 418SLD also disappeared; it had only been on sale for a year but had not sold well because of its poor performance. The 420GSi

Executive and 420GSi Sport went too, leaving the 420GSi and 420GSi Sport Turbo to pick up any disappointed customers. The number of diesel-engined models now went up to four, as the 418SD and 418SD Turbo catered for the cheaper end of the market alongside the existing 418SLD Turbo and 418GSD Turbo. For 1994 there were eight different models within the 400 range.

Other changes paralleled those made for the 200-series models at the same time. Side intrusion beams in the doors became standard. Ash Grey replaced Granite as the primary interior colour, with Stone Beige as an alternative for some body colours, and the seat fabrics changed. Driver's seats on SL trim derivatives now had height adjustment. Changes to the paint options were similar to those for the 200-series cars, remote central locking became standard (with Z-slot physical keys), and seven-spoke 15-inch alloy wheels with locking nuts became the norm. For the 420GSi Sport Turbo, there were now six-spoke 15-inch alloy wheels, inherited from the 220 Turbo Coupé.

There was then just one more set of changes during the 1994 model year. These came in March 1994 when a driver's side airbag became standard on SL models and above, and all models gained pre-tensioners for the front seat belts. At the same time, the 420GSi Sport Turbo became a plain 420GSi Turbo, though with no discernible changes. For those who cared, a retro-fit power steering kit became available in July for 1.4-litre cars which had not had PAS when new, exactly as it did for the 200-series cars.

### The Last 400s: 1995

The new 400-series cars of the HH-R range were scheduled for introduction in May 1995, which left rather less than a full season for production of the R8 types. Nevertheless, the full eleven-model range remained available as 1995 models, and the last examples were probably built at Longbridge in the early months of 1995. No doubt production of the low-volume types, such as the 420GSi Turbo, was wound down first, leaving the more mundane (but strong-selling) types in production until the end. Even then, the original 400 did not really die, because its Tourer derivative (see chapter 8) would remain in production for another three years.

## Technical Specifications, Rover 400 Saloon

### Engines

1396cc K-series 16-valve with single-point injection; 95PS, or 92PS for catalyst versions (414 models to 1992).

1396cc K-series 16-valve with multi-point injection; 103PS (414 models from 1992).

1590cc Honda D16A6 SOHC; 116PS (416 models, except GTi).

1590cc Honda D16A8 DOHC; 130PS (416GTi), or 124PS (416GTi automatic).

1769cc Peugeot XUD7TE turbocharged diesel; 88PS (418SLD Turbo, 418GSD Turbo, and 418SD Turbo).

1905cc Peugeot XUD9A diesel; 67PS (418SLD and 418SD).

1994cc M16 DOHC; 136PS (420 models, to 1993).

1994cc T16 DOHC; 136PS (420 models, from 1993).

1994cc T16 DOHC turbocharged; 200PS (420GSi Sport Turbo and 420GSi Turbo).

## Gearboxes

Five-speed Rover-Peugeot R65 manual (414 models) – Ratios: 3.417:1, 1.947:1, 1.333:1, 1.054:1, 0.854:1, reverse 3.583:1.

Five-speed Rover-Honda PG1 (all naturally aspirated diesels) – Ratios: 3.250:1, 1.894:1, 1.222:1, 0.935:1, 0.764:1, reverse 3.000:1.

Five-speed Rover-Honda PG1 (all turbodiesels) – Ratios: 3.166:1, 1.842:1, 1.222:1, 0.848:1, 0.648:1, reverse 3.000:1.

Five-speed Honda PP7A-53 manual (416 models, except GTi) – Ratios: 3.250:1. 1.894:1, 1.259:1, 0.937:1, 0.771:1, reverse 3.153:1.

Five-speed Honda PP7A-M4 manual (416GTi) – Ratios: 3.250:1, 1.944:1, 1.346:1, 1.044:1, 0.848:1, reverse 3.153:1.

Four-speed Honda E4 automatic (416 auto, except GTi) – Ratios: 2.705:1. 1.560:1. 1.027:1, 0.780:1, reverse 1.954:1.

Four-speed Honda E5 automatic (416GTi) – Ratios: 2.705:1, 1.560:1, 1.085:1, 0.825:1, reverse 1.954:1.

## Axle Ratio

3.937:1 (414, 418 diesel).
4.062:1 (418 turbodiesel).
4.200:1 (420).
4.214:1 (416 automatic).
4.250:1 (416GTi).
4.437:1 (416 manual).

## Suspension

Front independent suspension with MacPherson struts, forward facing tie bar and anti-roll bar. Rear independent suspension with double wishbones and compensating trailing arm; anti-roll bar on 416, 418 and 420.

## Steering

Manual or power-assisted Positive Centre Feel type.

## Brakes

414: 238 mm (9.4-in.) front discs and 203 mm (8.0-in.) rear drum.

416, 418 and 420 (and 414 with ABS option): 262 mm (10.3-in.) ventilated front discs and 239 mm (9.4-in.) solid rear discs. Bosch ABS 2E optional on 214, 418 and 420; Honda ALB2 on 416.

## Dimensions

| | |
|---|---|
| Overall length: | 4365 mm (171.8-in.). |
| Overall width: | 1940 mm (76.4-in.) over mirrors, 1680 mm (66.1-in.) excluding mirrors. |
| Overall height: | 1400 mm (55.1-in.). |
| Wheelbase: | 2550 mm (100.4-in.). |
| Track, front: | 1475 mm (58.1-in.). |
| Track, rear: | 1470 mm (57.8 in.). |

## Wheels and Tyres

414, 416 (except GTi), and 418: 5J x 14 steel wheels (5.5J x 14 alloys optional), 175/65TR14 radial tyres (185/60 x 14 optional).

416GTi: 5.5J x 14 alloy wheels, 185/60 x 14 radial tyres.

420: 5J x 14 steel wheels (5.5J x 15 alloys optional), 175/70HR14 radial tyres.

420GSi: 5.5J x 15 alloy wheels, 185/55VR15 radial tyres.

420 Turbo: 5.5J x 15 alloy wheels, 195/55ZR15 radial tyres.

## Kerb Weight

| | |
|---|---|
| 414Si | 1020 kg (2249 lb). |
| 414SLi | 1040 kg (2293 lb). |
| 416GSi | 1075 kg (2370 lb). |
| 416GSi automatic | 1095 kg (2415 lb). |
| 416GTi | 1100 kg (2425 lb). |
| 416GTi automatic | 1120 kg (2469 lb). |
| 418 | 1150 kg (2535 lb). |
| 418 Turbo | 1175 kg (2590 lb). |
| 420 SLi | 1165 kg (2570 lb). |
| 420GSi | 1175 kg (2590 lb). |
| 420 Turbo | 1215 kg (2678 lb). |

## Performance

Max speed:

| | |
|---|---|
| 414: | 106 mph. |
| 416: | 120 mph. |
| 416GTi: | 124 mph. |
| 418: | 96 mph. |
| 418 Turbo: | 106 mph. |
| 420: | 126 mph. |
| 420 Turbo: | 146 mph. |

0–60 mph:

| | |
|---|---|
| 414: | 11.1 sec. |
| 416: | 9.2 sec./10.8 sec. (automatic). |
| 416 GTi: | 8.6 sec./10.3 sec. (automatic). |
| 418: | 16.0 sec. |
| 418 Turbo: | 11.8 sec. |
| 420: | 8.1 sec. |
| 420 Turbo: | 6.4 sec. |

# CHAPTER 6

# The 200 Cabriolet (1992–1996)

The terms of the agreement between Rover and Honda allowed each party to develop the core R8 vehicle as it saw fit after the basic engineering had been completed, and Rover had every intention of making maximum use of the R8 platform, so during 1988 the company began work on the first of several derivatives. The first of these was a Cabriolet, which could relatively simply be produced from the structure of the three-door 200 series and was intended as a rival for the successful Cabriolet derivatives of cars like the VW Golf and Vauxhall Astra.

The development project for the Cabriolet was given the name of Tracer within Rover, and was led by Nick Fell, who would later transfer to the Land Rover side of the business and lead the Tempest (Discovery Series II) project. It belonged to mainstream R8 engineering, although many commentators have repeated the idea that the Cabriolet came from Rover Special Products, which in fact was not formed until a couple of years after work had begun on Project Tracer.

Essentially, the roof and upper body structure of the three-door R8 shell had to be removed, and torsional strength was then restored by underbody reinforcement and by a sturdy rollover bar. The convertible roof was designed to be manually operated as standard, but a power option was made available on all models at extra cost and was later standard on some; there were also gas struts to aid opening and closing. All production Cabriolets had split-fold rear seats and a special demister fan for the removable rear window in the convertible roof.

Some work was done on a removable hardtop for Project Tracer, but it soon became apparent that an additional model with a permanent hardtop – a Coupé – was a more attractive option. As a result, Project Tomcat was established to develop such a car. Its story is told in chapter 7.

The 200 Cabriolet was announced at the Geneva Motor Show in March 1992 and went on sale in Britain in April. Just three models were available – a 214 with Rover's K-series engine, and a Honda-engined twin-cam 216 with either manual or extra-cost automatic gearbox. It appears that the 2-litre M16 engine had also been tried but was ruled out because it led to an unacceptable level of scuttle-shake, which was already quite noticeable on the 1.4-litre and 1.6-litre models. All models came with burr walnut facia inserts, and the rollover bar had adjustable upper seat belt mounts, an interior light, and grab handles for the rear passengers. The tonneau cover was matched to the interior trim, which on the first cars was either Granite (grey) or Stone Beige.

The 200 Cabriolet was a very neat derivative of the three-door model and did not sacrifice too much interior space to the need for a hood well. The roll-over hoop blended well into the design, although it was a necessity both to restore body rigidity and to provide roll-over protection.

*Above*: The Cabriolet was not quite as good looking with the top up and suffered from quite large blind rear quarters. Nevertheless, in closed form it provided quite high levels of refinement.

*Left*: The interior was very much that of the three-door saloon R8, with that discreet use of wood trim that Rover always did so well to the annoyance of rival manufacturers! This one has the fabric upholstery option.

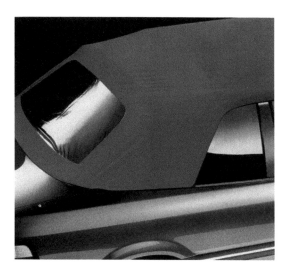

*Above*: Tail badges were minimal, the important part being that the car had a 16-valve engine! This is another picture of a very early car, dating from October 1991, but used for launch publicity in March 1992.

*Right*: Cabriolets came with a quick-fit 'get-you-home' hood for weather emergencies. It folded away into a stowage bag and could be kept in the boot.

A height-adjustable driver's seat was standard on both models, along with integral rear-seat head restraints. The 214 Cabriolet came with Windsor fabric upholstery and could be ordered with electric front windows and a power-operated radio aerial at extra cost. The 216 Cabriolet came as standard with Silverstone 'half-leather' sports-style front seats, electric front windows, and power-assisted steering. Both models could be ordered with ABS brakes and leather upholstery, the latter specially waterproofed. The Cabriolets were priced at the top end of the 200 range, and the 216 variant, with automatic gearbox, was briefly the most expensive 200 available, losing that distinction only when the Coupé models went on sale in October 1992.

Even though sales had begun in April 1992, many customers did not really become aware of the Cabriolet's existence until it was more widely publicised in connection with the NEC Motor Show that opened on 20 October. To make maximum impact Rover had prepared for the show a special concept model based on a 216 Cabriolet. This was known as the Liberty Design Concept, and was designed in collaboration with Liberty's, the London luxury fabric store.

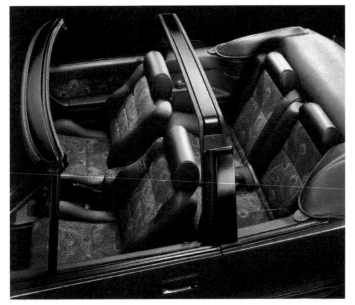

*Above*: The Cabriolet was already nearly six months old by the time of the 1992 Motor Show, and so Rover added a little excitement to its presentation by showing the Liberty concept model with striking Amaranth paintwork.

*Left*: The Liberty concept car used this hugely attractive Liberty fabric for its upholstery. This picture also gives a clear view of the roll-over bar's shape, which was designed to help the Cabriolet roof fit snugly.

The car was distinguished by a body colour called Amaranth, which had a flip-flop effect between purple and blue, and the upholstery and door casings were in Liberty's Hera design with pigmented metallic leather for the seat bolsters. The bumper tops, rubbing strips and tonneau cover were all colour keyed to the body, and there was a 400-style front bumper. Inside, the special features were a gold Liberty motif, a bird's-eye maple facia insert, an analogue clock in the centre console with a wood surround, and a leather-trimmed steering wheel. Whether there was ever any serious plan to put such a model into production is debatable, and a Rover insider has suggested that the cost of using the Liberty's materials would have made it prohibitively expensive.

All the first year's production of Cabriolets had a front end with only an air intake slot, but from November 1993 they had the chrome Rover grille that became standard on all 200 derivatives. Rover took the opportunity to make several other specification adjustments, adding what they called a sports front bumper in the body colour with a black finish above the chrome insert and changing some paint and interior colour options. Remote central locking now became standard, so the door lock was deleted from the passenger's side; there were also new 'Z-slot' locks and matching keys for the door and ignition. On the inside the sports seats from the 216 Cabriolet now became standard on the 214 Cabriolet as well.

Like the other R8 models, the Cabriolets were given a makeover in March 1994. The plain 214 Cabriolet went out of production and was replaced by a 214 Special Edition Cabriolet, which came as standard with the earlier options of a power-operated hood, electric front windows and an electric aerial. Front seat belt pre-tensioners were now standard on all Cabriolets, and so was a driver's side airbag. Seven-spoke alloy wheels distinguished the

The earliest Cabriolets had the original nose design with a simple slot-like air intake. This picture probably shows a pre-production car, as it is dated October 1991, although it was not issued to the press until the Cabriolet was announced in March 1992.

The Cabriolet with its new nose. This publicity picture was issued in November 1993 and shows a 216 model with the Rover grille and the black-topped 'sports' bumper. Rover clearly believed that British Racing Green looked good on the Cabriolet!

Green again! This picture was issued to publicise the March 1994 launch of the 214 SE Cabriolet, although there is nothing visible here to distinguish it from the earlier 1994 model cars.

In Germany, the Cabriolet was promoted with a limited edition when the new Rover grille was fitted. Although this picture is dated June 1993, it shows what would be a 1994 model. For Germany, the 216i Cabriolet came with leather upholstery.

Pictured in a setting that suggests the Netherlands rather than Germany, the 216i Cabriolet shows its attractive lines. The wheels on this limited edition were the usual seven-spoke alloys.

Special Edition, which came in British Racing Green, Nightfire Red or Tahiti Blue, with either Ash Grey or Stone Beige interior trim.

By the end of 1994 the Special Edition had gone, and the choice again rested between the 214 Cabriolet and 216 Cabriolet. Prices had increased, but there was an interesting special offer (also available on the Coupés) between 1 January and 31 March 1995, which provided the customer with a year's free insurance on a new Cabriolet.

Although the mainstream R8 models went out of production at the end of 1995, giving way to the new R3 or third-generation 200-series cars, the Cabriolet remained in production. Rover reasoned that, like the 200 Coupé and 400 Tourer, it was a niche model that could continue to sell alongside the new R3 types, which came only as three-door or five-door saloons, and as a result the Cabriolet was further developed over the next few years.

The next round of changes was announced on 22 March 1996. The new third-generation 200 models were now on sale after their announcement in autumn 1995, and so the 200 Cabriolet – clearly not related to the latest 200 series – was renamed simply Rover Cabriolet. The 1.4-litre model was dropped, and the four-model line-up now consisted of a Cabriolet 1.6 and a Cabriolet 1.6SE, each available with an automatic gearbox. The SE models were distinguished by a power-operated roof, leather upholstery, and six-spoke alloy wheels.

However, the power trains were now very different from before. In place of the earlier Honda 1.6-litre engine came the much less powerful 1.6-litre K-series engine, and the automatic gearbox was now a Volvo (DAF) CVT type, as used in the new R3 200-series cars. There was a loss of performance all round except on the CVT automatic, which actually accelerated faster than its predecessor; to some extent, this was masked by revised suspension settings that gave the cars a sportier feel. Side intrusion beams in the doors were also added, and the Amaranth pearlescent flip-flop paint previewed on the Liberty concept in 1992 was now added to the regular paint options list.

There were several differences in the passenger cabin, too, where (like all three R8 niche models) the Cabriolet now came with the dashboard from the latest Rover 200, complete with twin airbags as standard and a remote display for the radio and clock. As the two cars shared a bulkhead structure, this was a straightforward fit. Again, like the other niche models, the Cabriolet now came as standard with Piccadilly interior trim, with ash, green, or red fabric. There was a smokestone leather option, too, and all Cabriolets had front seat belt pre-tensioners and an ICE system with steering wheel controls

These were the last major changes made to the Cabriolets. Sales actually increased, and by July 1997 Rover were claiming that Cabriolet sales had gone up by 22 per cent during the calendar year. Capitalising on this, perhaps, Hawaiian Blue metallic now became a new paint option. And so it remained until the last Rover Cabriolet was built in summer 1998, some three years after the mainstream R8 200s on which it was based.

The third-phase models introduced in March 1996 all had the 1.6-litre K-series engine and were known simply as Rover Cabriolets. The new dashboard can be seen here, with a very attractive two-tone interior featuring red fabric.

The Cabriolet sold quite well outside Britain, too. This late example was pictured in New Zealand, and has the leather upholstery option with six-spoke alloy wheels.

The Cabriolets began to attract enthusiast owners some time before the mainstream R8 models, and this 1996 model was pictured at a classic car event. The interior is in two-tone grey fabric and the wheels are six-spoke alloys. (*Kieran White/WikiMedia Commons*)

## Technical Specifications, Rover Cabriolet

### Engine
1396cc K-series 16-valve with multi-point injection; 103PS (214 models).
1590cc Honda D16A8 DOHC; 122PS (216 models to 1996).
1589cc Rover K-series 16-valve with multi-point injection; 111PS (from 1996).

### Gearbox
Five-speed R65 manual (214) – Ratios: 3.417:1, 1.947:1, 1.333:1, 1.054:1, 0.854:1, reverse 3.583:1.
Five-speed Honda PP7A-53 manual (216) – Ratios: 3.250:1. 1.894:1, 1.259:1, 0.937:1, 0.771:1, reverse 3.153:1.
Four-speed Honda E4 automatic (216 auto with Honda engine) – Ratios: 2.705:1. 1.560:1. 1.027:1, 0.780:1, reverse 1.954:1.
CVT automatic (1.6 auto with K-series engine).

### Axle Ratio
3.937:1 (214).
4.214:1 (216 automatic).
4.437:1 (216).

### Suspension
Front independent suspension with MacPherson struts, forward facing tie bar and anti-roll bar. Rear independent suspension with double wishbones and compensating trailing arm; anti-roll bar on 216.

## Steering

Positive Centre Feel type; unassisted on 214 to March 1994, or power-assisted on all 216 models and 214SE.

## Brakes

214: 238 mm (9.4-in.) front discs and 203 mm (8.0-in.) rear drums.

216 (and 214 with ABS option): 262 mm (10.3-in.) ventilated front discs and 239 mm (9.4-in.) solid rear discs. Bosch ABS 2E optional on 214 and 216 from 1996; Honda ALB2 on 216 to 1996.

## Dimensions

| | |
|---|---|
| Overall length: | 4218 mm (166.1-in.). |
| Overall width: | 1940 mm (76.4-in.) over mirrors, 1680 mm (66.1-in.) excluding mirrors. |
| Overall height: | 1389 mm (54.7-in.). |
| Wheelbase: | 2550mm (100.4-in.). |
| Track, front: | 1480 mm (58.3-in.). |
| Track, rear: | 1470 mm (57.8-in.). |

## Wheels and Tyres

5J x 14 steel wheels (214 and 216) 175/65HR14 radial tyres, 5.5J x 15 alloy wheels (1.6SE) 185/5VR15 radial tyres.

## Kerb Weight

| | |
|---|---|
| 214: | 1075 kg (2370 lb). |
| 216: | 1135 kg (2500 lb). |

## Performance

Max speed:

| | |
|---|---|
| 214 | 104 mph. |
| 216 (Honda) | 120 mph/117 mph (automatic). |
| 216 (K-series) | 115 mph/112 mph (automatic). |

0–60 mph:

| | |
|---|---|
| 214: | 11.8 sec. |
| 216 (Honda): | 9.0 sec./10.8 sec. (automatic). |
| 216 (K-series): | 9.7 sec./10.2 sec. (automatic). |

# CHAPTER 7

# The 200 'Tomcat' Coupé (1992–1998)

The Tomcat Coupé brought glamour and excitement to the Rover range, and when launched in 1992 became the second of the special R8 derivatives to reach production. As chapter 6 explains, its origins lay in some work done to design a removable hardtop for the Project Tracer Cabriolet, which by 1989 had become an independent project to design a Coupé. This was known as Project Tomcat and, like the Tracer Cabriolet, it was led by Nick Fell within the mainstream R8 engineering group. Rover's aim was to compete with existing compact sports Coupés such as the highly successful VW Scirocco.

An early idea for the Tracer Cabriolet was to add removable rear windows and roof panels to the Cabriolet body. A full-size mock-up demonstrated that painting the rollover bar to match the bodyshell instead of in the contrasting black used for the Cabriolet helped the two cars look more different. At the time it was made, one idea was to make the R8-based Coupé into a new MG sports model, and so the mock-up wore MG branding. However, the success of the 1989 Mazda MX-5 roadster prompted Rover to save the MG name for a new sports roadster – which was released as the MGF in 1995.

Early in the Tomcat project there were thoughts of giving the car MG badges, and this full-size mock-up was photographed wearing them. At this stage, there was a wide central hoop and the rear window treatment differed from the eventual production design. *(David Knowles Collection)*

The production Coupé was nevertheless still a stunning-looking car. This early example in Flame Red was new in December 1992. *(Ian Bone)*

So the design developed as a derivative of the Rover range, and much of the credit for the strikingly attractive two-door sports Coupé that entered production must go to Chris Greville-Smith in the Rover Design Studio. Still based on the floorpan and underpinnings of the three-door R8, the Tomcat Coupé had very different lines from the other R8 models. It was sleek and curvaceous, and its otherwise conventional fixed roof contained a sunroof with two tilt-or-remove glass panels separated by a T-bar that could also be removed and stowed in the boot in a special protective cover. The semi-reflective glass in those sunroof panels was coated with titanium, which dispensed with the need for a sun blind by restricting the transmission of solar heat to just 6 per cent.

As top models of the Tomcat were always intended to have the 2-litre T16 engine, a bonnet was designed with a blister to give clearance for that engine's cambelt cover. For production, the 'power bulge' bonnet would be standardised on all models, even though the bulge was not only redundant when the 1.6-litre Honda engine was fitted but was actually faintly ridiculous, as the cambelt of the Honda engine was on the other side of the car altogether!

The Tomcat Coupé was scheduled for launch in early October 1992, and over that summer the team that had worked on the project suggested using one to establish some speed records at the Millbrook proving ground, in Bedfordshire, in advance of the launch itself. This suited the Rover publicity department very well: if the attempt was successful, it would generate valuable media coverage, and if it failed to achieve its aims, it could be quietly forgotten.

Two examples of the 200 bhp 220 Coupé Turbo were prepared by an eighty-strong team of volunteers from Rover. The plan was to run them alongside one another in case one failed, and although mechanically standard, both were carefully fettled to give their best for the record runs. A first attempt over the weekend of 29–30 August claimed multiple shorter-distance records, but the attempt on the 24-hour record was aborted because of an oil starvation problem. A second attempt on 26–27 September was successful, when

The rear treatment was very effective, and identification was minimal, with just the Rover Viking ship and a discreet 'turbo' badge. The bootlid and under-bumper spoilers gave a subtly purposeful look to the car.

The car was initially known as the 220 Coupé Turbo, and this underbonnet picture shows the original M-series turbocharged 2-litre engine. (*Ian Bone*)

*Above left*: The interior was recognisably R8, but had a clear sporting look that was entirely in keeping with the car's purpose. *(Ian Bone)*

*Above right*: Less visible in some paint colours than in others, this is the bonnet 'bulge' that was made standard on all the Coupés, whether the engine underneath needed it or not.

the car stopped only for refuelling and driver changes, and covered a total of 3,322 miles. The two attempts broke a total of thirty-seven existing records, including 22 in Class E (for 1500–2000cc cars) and fifteen outright UK records. The Coupé reached a maximum speed of 156 mph and recorded an average of 138 mph over the twenty-four hours.

That made for an impressive debut when the car was introduced at the Paris Salon on 6 October. There were three models available, starting with a 216 Coupé with the 111PS

*Above*: Just before the launch of the Coupé in 1992, a mechanically standard 2-litre model took a series of speed records. The car was pictured outside the Rover Group's Gaydon test centre in Warwickshire.

*Left*: ...and here is the proof of one of those records, in this case for the 5 kilometres flying start, over which the car achieved an average of 156 mph. *(John Batchelor)*

single-cam Honda engine. With the standard manual gearbox (an automatic was optional), this gave the car a top speed of 120 mph with 0–60 mph acceleration in 9.5 seconds. All the 1.6-litre models had alloy wheels, and Rover expected them to account for 45 per cent of Coupé sales.

Next up, and also expected to account for 45 per cent of sales, was a 220 Coupé, which was visually distinguished by a boot-mounted spoiler. This was the first R8 model to have the latest 136PS T16 2-litre engine that was a further development of the M16 seen in the 220GTi three-door cars. However, it was completely eclipsed by the top model 220 Coupé Turbo, which had a turbocharged T16 engine and 200PS.

The flagship 220 Coupé Turbo was the fastest and most powerful production car ever to carry Rover badges. It could reach 60 mph from rest in 6.2 seconds and had a maximum speed of 150 mph, which added up to giant-killing performance for 1992. The gearbox was a five-speed PG1 type, and to keep all that power in check in a front-wheel-drive car, there were wider tyres and a torsen (torque-sensing) differential that was designed to prevent torque steer under hard acceleration (although in practice it was not wholly effective at doing so). This differential was also made optional on the naturally aspirated 220 Coupé.

When the Coupés were introduced to Britain at the NEC Motor Show that opened on 13 October, they were accompanied on the show stand by the record-breaking 220 Coupé Turbo. Its production equivalent immediately became the most expensive R8 derivative, and the other models were also priced high up the scale. All these first models had the 200-series style of nose, with an air intake slot and no grille. The 1.6-litre cars had the seven-spoke alloy wheels available on some other R8 models, but the two 2-litre models variants came with chunkier-looking six-spoke alloys.

There were three solid colours (Black, Flame Red, and White Diamond), three metallics (Nordic Blue, Polynesian Turquoise, and Quicksilver), and two pearlescent paints. Nightfire Red was one of the most attractive Rover colours ever, and the second pearlescent was new with the Coupés and exclusive to them; it was called Tahiti Blue. Ash Grey was the primary interior colour option, but Stone Beige could be had with some colours. Upholstery was in Silverstone velour on the 216 and in Silverstone with leather bolsters on both the 2-litre models, while all variants could be ordered with an all-leather option at extra cost. Burr walnut contributed a Rover ambience, and all models had a practical split-fold rear seat.

The 2-litre cars had six-spoke alloy wheels, but the Honda-engined 216 models had the seven-spoke type pictured here on an early car.

Rover hoped they might interest police forces in the 220 Coupé Turbo, and prepared one as a demonstrator. It was pictured while on loan to London's Metropolitan Police – but no order followed. *(Police Vehicle Enthusiasts' Club)*

### What the Press Thought

Generally, the press reacted very favourably to the Coupés. For *The Independent* newspaper of 24 October 1992, Roger Bell tried a 220 Turbo Coupé and described the Coupés as 'stylish, clean-cut cars that just pass muster as four-seaters, even though the roof is low at the back, and leg-room tight. Children are easily accommodated, beanpoles are not.'

Bell liked the 'clean surge' of power from the turbocharged engine, but he had some reservations about the torsen differential, which 'does not completely eliminate wheelspin on wet roads or steering tug when aggressive, first-gear starts are attempted.' Overall, 'if it is not pushed to boy-racer limits, the 220 Turbo is a pleasant, easy car to drive. The chassis and hard-riding suspension handle 200 horsepower with impunity; so do the strong brakes. You never feel less than secure in this powerful car. But it takes more than the promise of 150 mph to make an uplifting motoring experience. That magic fluency – the ability to flow through bends rather than steer round them – is not quite there.'

When *Autocar & Motor* compared a 216 Coupé with a Vauxhall Calibra coupé in their issue of 18 November 1992, they wrote that 'the Rover feels quicker than it has any right to with only 111 bhp to propel it ... [but] to keep the 216 bubbling at its best, you have to use all the gears. If you don't, the Honda-derived engine all too readily falls away from its power peak at a busy but sonically stimulating 6300 rpm.' The absence of torque-steer made its steering better than that of the 220 Turbo Coupé, but 'the promisingly crisp turn-in is all but spoilt by the linear and lifeless responses once the car is committed to a bend.' Brakes were 'a mite snatchy under light application, yet peculiarly spongy under heavier loads', the boot was too small, and 'there isn't enough head and legroom for tall drivers.' They preferred the Vauxhall.

### The 1994 and 1995 Cars

For the next two years the model line-up of 216, 220 and 220 Turbo remained unchanged, but from November 1993 all the Coupés took on the chromed Rover grille that was now standard across the R8 range, and there were some changes to the colour options.

All models now came with height adjustment for the driver's seat, and with remote central locking. As on other R8s, the door lock was deleted from the passenger's side, and there were new 'Z-slot' locks and matching keys for the door and ignition. But there were cost savings, too, as the dashboard lighting dimmer and ignition keylock light were deleted, and the amount of interior leather was reduced in those models which had it. Seats remained Ash Grey, with Stone Beige as an alternative for some body colours.

For the 1994 season, Rover also arranged a promotional one-marque race series for the 220 Turbo Coupé. This was known as the Dunlop Rover Turbo Cup and was held at venues in the UK and Europe, where the races provided support attractions to the main event.

*Above*: The 1994 model Coupés took on the new Rover grille that was rolled out across the R8 range. The six-spoke alloy wheels make clear that this one, pictured for release to the press, was a 220 Turbo Coupé.

*Right*: During 1994, Coupés featured in a one-make race series called the Dunlop Rover Turbo Cup. This promotional sticker for the series gives a good idea of how the cars looked.

A total of thirty-six cars were specially prepared for this series, which lasted for only one season but successfully made its point that the Coupé was an exciting high-performance car. After the 1994 season, the series evolved into the Stafford Landrover Super Coupé Cup, in which the Rovers continued to race for a time. Many of the original Turbo Cup series cars still survive today in club racing.

Further production changes occurred in March 1994, when all Coupés were given the driver's airbag and seat belt pre-tensioners that became standard on other R8 derivatives at the same time. By this time, Rover was already planning to replace the Honda 1.6-litre engine with a K-series unit of similar capacity, and so the company gave some thought to disposing of stocks of the old-model 216 Coupés in advance of the introduction of their replacements.

The first move was an incentive purchase programme, shared with the Cabriolets, which offered a year's free insurance on cars purchased between 1 January and 31 March 1995. The second stage was to make the 216 models more attractive, and to that end Rover introduced a 216SE derivative, distinguished visually by the addition of a rear spoiler (from the 220 models) and front fog lamps.

## The 1996 Revisions

In practice, the Honda-engined cars remained in production for several more months. They were not replaced in the showrooms until the end of March 1996, at which point the Coupé range was completely overhauled.

The major changes were to the engines. Both the Honda 1.6 and the Rover T16 types were replaced by the latest 'big K' versions of the K-series. There were three models in the new line-up, all with new names; as with the Cabriolets, Rover wanted to break the connection with the 200 series because that range had now been replaced by a new car. There was now a Rover Coupé 1.6, a Rover Coupé 1.6 Automatic, and a Rover Coupé 1.8 VVC, all with revised suspension settings to suit minor changes in the weight distribution.

The new 1.6-litre engine made little difference to the performance available from the smaller-engined Coupés, although the optional automatic gearbox was now a CVT type instead of the earlier conventional Honda automatic. The decision to drop the T16 engines and replace them with the new 1.8-litre VVC K-series was not such a good one, however, and also backfired quite badly.

For a start, the VVC (variable valve control) engine had only 145PS, which was more than the 136PS of the T16 in the older 220 Coupé but no match for the 200PS of the old 220 Coupé Turbo. Perhaps the well-known traction problems associated with that car had prompted Rover not to replace it directly. The second problem came about because of the success of the VVC engine in the new MGF roadster. Although Rover had promised to have VVC Coupés in the showrooms by summer 1996, in practice they had to defer availability until 1997 because there were not enough VVC engines to go round.

There were major changes elsewhere, too. Like the Cabriolet and Tourer niche models, the Coupés took on a new dashboard similar to that of the latest R3 200-series cars. This brought airbags for both driver and passenger, and the ICE system now came with steering wheel controls and a remote display that doubled as a clock. Belt pre-tensioners were of course standard again, and the doors now incorporated side intrusion beams. The 1.6 models now had steel wheels with plastic trims as standard, but most were probably

In 1996, the 1.8-litre VVC engine replaced both the naturally aspirated and turbocharged 2-litre types, but availability of the new models was delayed. This one is in Amaranth, a flip-flop pearlescent paint.

ordered with the extra cost six-spoke alloy option. The 1.8 VVC models all had ABS and unique five-spoke alloys as standard.

There was a range of seven colours for these revised models, including the striking Amaranth purple-to-blue flip-flop pearlescent paint that was introduced on Cabriolets at the same time. The other colours were familiar: British Racing Green, Charcoal, Flame Red, Nightfire Red, Platinum and Tahiti Blue. Interiors shared revisions with the Cabriolets, too. Cloth was standard for the upholstery of the seat centres, in Ash Grey or Red; bolsters were trimmed in Piccadilly Grey cloth on the 1.6 but in leather on the 1.8 VVC, and both models could have smokestone leather at extra cost.

## The Final Cars

The 1.8 VVC models duly became available in 1997, and (perhaps as a consequence of this), the 1.6 models were revised at the start of July. Essentially, the price of the steel-wheeled base model was reduced, and a new 1.6 SE was introduced, with five-spoke alloy wheels, a body-coloured rear spoiler, and integral fog lamps.

Further minor revisions were made towards the end of production, when Diamond White was reintroduced, and a few cars were painted in the new colour of Anthracite. However, there were no further changes of note until Rover withdrew the Coupés in summer 1998. They were not directly replaced in the Rover range.

# Technical Specifications, Rover Coupé

## Engines
1590cc Honda SOHC; 111PS.
1994cc Rover T16 DOHC; 136PS.
1994cc Rover T16 turbocharged DOHC; 200PS.
1589cc Rover K-series 16-valve with multi-point injection; 111PS (from 1996).
1796cc Rover K-series 16-valve with multi-point injection; 145PS (from 1996).

## Gearboxes
Five-speed Honda PP7A-53 (216) – Ratios: 3.250:1. 1.894:1, 1.259:1, 0.937:1, 0.771:1, reverse 3.153:1.
Five-speed Rover-Honda PG1 (1.6, 220 and 1.8VVC) – Ratios: 2.923:1, 1.750:1, 1.220:1, 0.935:1, 0.765:1, reverse 3.000:1.
Four-speed Honda E4 automatic (216 auto with Honda engine) – Ratios: 2.705:1. 1.560:1. 1.027:1, 0.780:1, reverse 1.954:1.
CVT automatic (1.6 auto with K-series engine).

## Axle Ratio
4.214:1 (216 automatic).
4.200:1 (220 and 1.8).
4.437:1 (216).

## Suspension
Front independent suspension with MacPherson struts, forward facing tie bar and anti-roll bar. Rear independent suspension with double wishbones, compensating trailing arm and anti-roll bar.

## Steering
Positive Centre Feel type; power-assisted on all models.

## Brakes
216 and 1.6: 262 mm (10.3-in.) ventilated front discs and 239 mm (9.4-in.) solid rear discs. ABS (Honda ALB2) optional on 216 models; Bosch ABS 2E optional on 1.6 (K-series) models and standard on 220, 220 Turbo and 1.8VVC.

## Dimensions
| | |
|---|---|
| Overall length: | 4270 mm (168.1-in.). |
| Overall width: | 1940 mm (76.4-in.) over mirrors, 1680 mm (66.1-in.) excluding mirrors. |
| Overall height: | 1369 mm (53.9-in.). |
| Wheelbase: | 2550 mm (100.4-in.). |
| Track, front: | 1480 mm (58.3-in.). |
| Track, rear: | 1470 mm (57.8-in.). |

## Wheels and Tyres

216, 1.6 SE (K-series) and 1.8 VVC: 5.5J x 15 alloy wheels, 185/55VR15 radial tyres. 220 models: 5.5J x 15 alloy wheels, 185/55VR15 radial tyres (220 Coupé), 195/55ZR15 radial tyres (220 Turbo Coupé). 1.6 (K-series): 5J x 15 steel wheels, 195/55HR15 radial tyres.

## Kerb Weight

| | |
|---|---|
| 216: | 1080 kg (2380 lb). |
| 216 (auto): | 1100 kg (2425 lb). |
| 220: | 1165 kg (2570 lb). |
| 220 Turbo: | 1185 kg (2610 lb). |
| 1.6 (K-series): | 1090 kg (2400 lb). |
| 1.8 VVC: | 1090 kg (2400 lb). |

## Performance

Max speed:

| | |
|---|---|
| 216: | 120 mph. |
| 216 (automatic): | 118 mph. |
| 220: | 127 mph. |
| 220 Turbo: | 150 mph. |
| 1.6: | 120 mph. |
| 1.8 VVC: | 131 mph. |

0–60 mph:

| | |
|---|---|
| 216: | 9.5 sec. |
| 216 (auto): | 11.2 sec. |
| 220: | 8.2 sec. |
| 220 Turbo: | 6.2 sec. |
| 1.6: | 9.5 sec. |
| 1.8 VVC: | 7.8 sec. |

CHAPTER 8

# The 400 Tourer (1994–1998)

As a reaction to the popularity of 'people carriers' like the Renault Espace, the later 1980s saw an increase of the numbers of small estate cars on the market. These estates were not intended as big load carriers but were ideal for owners who wanted to transport dogs, or to carry a limited amount of sporting kit; obvious examples were the BMW 3-series Touring and the Audi 80 Avant. They became known as 'lifestyle' estates, and Rover determined to develop a competitor from the R8 platform.

So, Project Tex became the third niche variant of the R8, and this time its development was entrusted to the new Rover Special Products team. Although it was always intended as the flagship variant of the R8 range, Rover never expected it to become a big seller, and in fact production was deliberately limited to just 220 cars a week when it went on sale in 1994.

Some careful marketing was associated with this car. It was aligned with the 400 range rather than the 200 range and was promoted as a sporty model with sharp styling and a luxurious interior – very much in contrast to the more capacious Montego estate, which was due to go out of production shortly. This image helped to justify the high prices asked for the Tourer, and although the top model was not as expensive as the top-of-the-range 420 GSi Turbo, it was certainly among the most expensive derivatives of the 400. More prosaically, perhaps, estate cars were generally expected to be derivatives of saloons rather than of hatchbacks, and so the link to the four-door saloons of the 400 range also satisfied customer expectations.

The 400 Tourer was the last of the niche R8 models to reach the showrooms, and was not released until the 1994 Geneva Show, which opened on 4 March. The body styling was an entirely straightforward adaptation of the 400 saloon with a top-hinged tailgate and an attractively rounded trailing edge to the third window on each side, plus a stylish raked radio aerial on the rear roof. The interior came only with the top two levels of equipment associated with the 400 range. Just four models were available: a 416SLi Tourer with the 111PS single-cam Honda engine; a 416SLi with automatic gearbox; a 418SLD Turbo with the 88PS turbocharged diesel; and a 420GSi with the 136PS T16 engine.

The Tourer was initially offered in a range of six colours, including just one solid option, three metallics, and two pearlescent options. Door mirror bodies were painted in the body colour, and the 420GSi came with seven-spoke alloy wheels as standard. The 420GSi also had a body-coloured rear appliqué panel and a chrome exhaust tailpipe finisher. All the petrol models came with larger front and rear anti-roll bars than their saloon cousins,

*Above*: This is a late Tourer with the K-series engine and plastic wheel trims designed to look like more expensive alloy wheels.

*Right*: The 400 Tourer was a good looking car from every angle, and there was no indication that the estate rear end had been grafted on as an afterthought. This 1994 press picture shows a 420GSi with the seven-spoke alloy wheels.

The 400 Tourer was sometimes described as a 'lifestyle' estate, and this publicity picture certainly lives up to that description. Although it was not a capacious load-lugger, it had enough space for the occasional long load, or (more regularly) for a dog.

to compensate for their extra weight. The 420GSi had rear disc brakes and ABS was an extra-cost option across the Tourer range.

The 1.6-litre and diesel models had the Granite-coloured Windsor velour upholstery associated with the SL trim level, but the 2-litre variants had sports-style seats with

*Above*: The rear seats could be folded down to extend the load space but, as this picture shows, the floor area behind them was no greater than in the comparable saloons.

*Left*: The 400 Tourer was always well equipped, even in entry level 1.6-litre form. This shows the driving compartment of a top-model 420GSi.

Ash Grey Silverstone fabric and leather bolsters. All models had a driver's airbag and pre-tensioners for the front seat belts from the start (these were introduced on other models in March 1994, as the Tourer was launched). They also had electric front windows, an electric sunroof, remote central door locking and both perimetric and volumetric anti-theft alarms together with an engine immobiliser. The driver's seat on all models had lumbar adjustment, and on the 420GSi the passenger's seat had it as well.

## Rover Special Products

Rover Special Products, or RSP, opened for business on 28 March 1990, although it had been in the making for some time before that. Its purpose was to develop new concepts that could become low-volume products alongside the mainstream Rover models, and to manage selected projects through to production. Fundamental to it was the idea of fast-tracking good ideas, and its inspiration was really the success of Project Jay, which was initiated in 1986 and, by using new working methods, delivered the hugely successful Land Rover Discovery in autumn 1989.

Rover embarked on a feasibility study for this new division at the start of 1990. The study demonstrated that it was wholly viable, and RSP was established within the Sales and Marketing division, which at that stage was run by Marketing Director Kevin Morley. It drew specialists from existing areas, including the concept studio that was run by former Ogle Design Director Richard Hamblin. Along with Hamblin, RSP had three further Directors. Steve Schlemmer looked after the Land Rover side, and David Wiseman and John Stephenson were each responsible for car concepts.

RSP worked by formulating new concepts, and then selecting the best to develop as engineering feasibility studies. To avoid impinging on mainstream design and engineering resources, projects were then outsourced to independent design consultancies, whose job was to develop them into prototypes. The prototypes would then be passed to the Rover (or Land Rover) engineers to be worked up as production models.

Unsurprisingly, the RSP system caused a certain amount of resentment among the mainstream Rover engineers, who often felt that they were being by-passed and the RSP team was unfairly receiving special treatment. RSP did not survive for long after the BMW takeover in January 1994, because the German company called for development resources to be focussed on mainstream products, but the division did produce some very interesting cars in its time. Two of those were developed from the R8 family, and they were the 220GTi and the 400 Tourer (Project Tex).

### The Later Tourers

When the second-generation Rover 400 range was introduced in 1995, it became very clear that the slickly styled Tourer was not derived from it. So it was no surprise when the '400' part of the name was dropped during 1996 and the R8 estate car became a plain Rover Tourer. The turning-point came in March, when the Tourer, like the other R8 niche models, was comprehensively overhauled.

On the mechanical side, the revised Tourers came with a new range of engines. The turbocharged diesel disappeared, and the 1.6-litre Honda engine gave way to a similarly powered 1.6-litre K-series, while the 2-litre T16 was to be replaced by the new 1.8-litre VVC version of the K-series. However, as happened with the Coupé, actual production of the VVC models was delayed because Rover needed all the engines it could make to meet demand for the MGF roadster. By the time engines did become available, Rover had

The rear section and tailgate were a very successful piece of design. This is a late 420GSi Tourer in Nightfire Red. (*Jeremy Howson*)

The Tourer appealed in export markets as well. This is a late model for Germany, in a press picture dated September 1995. Like other models with the 2.0-litre engine, the Tourer had a bonnet bulge when so equipped.

decided not to proceed with the model, and as a result only a handful of pre-production examples were ever built; the best guess is that about seven or eight were made in all.

These revised Tourers shared several changes with the other niche models. They came with the new dashboard from the R3 200 models, with airbags for both driver and passenger, they had side intrusion beams in the doors, and they had steel wheels as standard with trims from the earlier SLi models. Interior trim featured Piccadilly Grey seat bolsters with Ash or Geen wearing surfaces.

Rover gave a fillip to sales at the start of July 1997 by creating a new 1.6 SE model, exactly as they did for the Coupé. The SE Tourer gained six-spoke alloy wheels, half-leather seats, and a chrome tailpipe finisher. These final revisions then carried the Tourer through until production ended in summer 1998, and a 1.6-litre Tourer was the very last R8 to be built. Painted in Platinum Silver, it was later registered as S857 WOM. The car was originally retained in the Heritage Collection but was sold to a private owner at auction in 2003.

## Technical Specifications, Rover Tourer

*Engines*
1.6-litre (1589cc) Rover K-series four-cylinder, with 111PS.
1.6-litre (1590cc) Honda D-series four-cylinder, with 111PS.
1.8-litre (1769cc) Peugeot turbodiesel four-cylinder, with 88PS.
2.0-litre (1994cc) Rover T-series four-cylinder, with 136PS.

*Gearboxes*
Five-speed Honda PP7A-53 (1.6) – Ratios: 3.250:1. 1.894:1, 1.259:1, 0.937:1, 0.771:1, reverse 3.153:1.
Five-speed Rover-Honda PG1 (turbodiesel) – Ratios: 3.166:1, 1.842:1, 1.222:1, 0.848:1, 0.648:1, reverse 3.000:1.
Five-speed Rover-Honda PG1 (2.0) – Ratios: 2.923:1, 1.750:1, 1.222:1, 0.935:1, 0.764:1, reverse 3,000:1.
Four-speed Honda E4 automatic (1.6 auto) – Ratios: 2.705:1. 1.560:1. 1.027:1, 0.780:1, reverse 1.954:1.
CVT automatic (1.6 auto with K-series engine).

## Axle Ratio
4.062:1 (1.8 diesel).
4.200:1 (420).
4.214:1 (416 automatic).
4.437:1 (416).

## Suspension
Front independent suspension with MacPherson struts, forward facing tie bar and anti-roll bar. Rear independent suspension with double wishbones and compensating trailing arm.

## Steering
Power-assisted Positive Centre Feel type.

## Brakes
416 and 420: 262 mm (10.3-in.) ventilated front discs and 238 mm (9.4-in.) rear drums.
418: 262 mm (10.3-in.) ventilated front discs and 203 mm (8.0-in.) rear drums.
ABS optional on all models, with 239 mm (9.4-in.) solid rear discs.

## Dimensions
| | |
|---|---|
| Overall length: | 4370 mm (172.0-in.). |
| Overall width: | 1680 mm (66.1-in.) excluding mirrors. |
| Overall height: | 1400 mm (55.1-in.). |
| Wheelbase: | 2550 mm (100.4-in.). |
| Track, front: | 1480 mm (58.3-in.). |
| Track, rear: | 1470mm (57.8-in.). |

## Wheels and Tyres
416 and 418: 14-inch steel wheels with 175/65HR14 tyres.
420: 15-inch alloy wheels with 185/55VR15 tyres.

## Kerb weight
| | |
|---|---|
| 1.6: | 1150 kg (2535 lb). |
| 1.8 turbodiesel: | 1240 kg (2734 lb). |
| 2.0: | 1230 kg (2711 lb). |

## Performance
Max speed:
| | |
|---|---|
| 1.6: | 115 mph/112 mph (automatic). |
| 1.8 turbodiesel | 105 mph. |
| 2.0: | 122 mph. |

0–60mph:
| | |
|---|---|
| 1.6: | 10.5 sec./12.3 sec. (automatic). |
| 1.8 turbodiesel: | 13.2 sec. |
| 2.0: | 9.2 sec. |

# Chapter 9

# Appendix

## Colours and Trims

*Paint Colour Availability, 1990–1995 Model Years*

| (Model year:) | 1990 | 1991 | 1992 | 1993 | 1994 | 1995 |
|---|---|---|---|---|---|---|
| *Solids* | | | | | | |
| Black | ▓ | ▓ | ▓ | ▓ | | |
| Flame Red | ▓ | ▓ | ▓ | ▓ | ▓ | |
| Henley Blue | ▓ | ▓ | | | | |
| Midnight Blue | | | (1) | ▓ | ▓ | ▓ |
| Ocean Blue | | | | ▓ | ▓ | ▓ |
| Oyster Beige | ▓ | ▓ | ▓ | | | |
| White Diamond | ▓ | ▓ | ▓ | | | |
| *Metallics* | | | | | | |
| Amethyst | | | (1) | ▓ | ▓ | |
| Atlantic Blue | ▓ | ▓ | ▓ | ▓ | ▓ | ▓ |
| Azure Blue | ▓ | ▓ | ▓ | ▓ | | |
| British Racing Green | ▓ | ▓ | ▓ | ▓ | ▓ | ▓ |
| Charcoal | | | | | ▓ | ▓ |
| Lynx Bronze | ▓ | | | | | |
| Nordic Blue | | | (1) | | | |
| Polynesian Turquoise | | | (2) | (4) | (4) | |
| Pulsar Silver | ▓ | ▓ | ▓ | ▓ | ▓ | ▓ |
| Quicksilver | | | | ▓ | ▓ | ▓ |
| Steel Grey | ▓ | ▓ | | | | |
| Stone Grey | ▓ | | | | | |
| *Pearlescents* | | | | | | |
| Caribbean Blue | | | (3) | ▓ | ▓ | |
| Cherry Red | ▓ | ▓ | | | | |
| Nighfire Red | | | (1) | | | |
| Tahiti Blue | | | | (5) | ▓ | (7) |
| White Gold | | | | | (6) | |

(1) Not available on Cabriolet or Coupé models.

(2) Cabriolet only.

(3) Available only on 400 models and on 220GTi three-door models.

(4) Cabriolet and Coupé only.

(5) Coupé only.

(6) 200 three-door, five-door, and 400 saloon only.

(7) Not available on standard 200 models.

## 1996–1998 Model Years

All colours shown were available for all three model years.

| Solids | Cabriolet | Coupé | Tourer |
|---|---|---|---|
| Flame Red | ▓ | ▓ | |
| White Diamond | | | ▓ |
| Metallics | | | |
| British Racing Green | | | |
| Charcoal | ▓ | | |
| Platinum Silver | | | |
| Pearlescents | | | |
| Amaranth | ▓ | ▓ | |
| Nightfire Red | ▓ | | |
| Tahiti Blue | ▓ | ▓ | |

## Interior Colour and Trim Availability

*1990–1992 Model Years:*

Flint, Mink, or Prussian Blue (all cloth; leather optional on GSi models and standard on 416GTi).

*1992 Model Year:*

From November 1991 for 420GSi Sport. Lightning cloth with leather bolsters from January for 400. From April for 200: Flint or Stone Beige (all cloth; leather options as before).

*1993 Model Year:*

Granite or Stone Beige; renaissance cloth on SL and below; Chevron cloth on GS; lightning cloth with velour bolsters on GTi three-door. Lightning cloth with leather bolsters on GTi five-door, 220 three-doors, and 420GSi Sport. Leather on 420GSi Executive; optional on other 420GSi models.

*1994 Model Year:*

Ash Grey or Stone Beige; Renaissance on Si and below; Windsor on SL and above; Silverstone with leather on GSi three-door; leather available on SL and above, except on 218SLD Turbo.

*1995 Model Year:*

Granite cloth on standard models; Ash Grey cloth for sporty and SEi models. Leather availability as for 1994.

*1996–1997 Model Years:*

Ash Grey or Red for Cabriolet and Coupé; Ash Grey or Green for Tourer Piccadilly cloth.

*1998 Model Year:*

Ash Grey or Red for Cabriolet and Coupé; Ash Grey or Green for Tourer; Piccadilly cloth with leather bolsters for 1.8 VVC Coupé. Leather option for Coupé and Tourer.

# CHAPTER 10

# Acknowledgements

Putting together this brief history of a very complex range has been made much easier by considerable input from a number of people. To basic information provided by my own observation and by Rover's press releases and sales brochures, I've been able to add valuable insights from members of the Rover 200 & 400 Owners' Club (www.rover200.org. uk). Special thanks go to Jeremy Howson, who painstakingly combed my drafts for errors, and to John Batchelor, who was involved with the cars' development.

Many pictures used here came from the Rover Press Office, and my thanks go to Denis Chick and Kevin Jones, who were responsible for most of the press releases and who are still happy to talk about Rover days. Thanks, too, to owners James Mclernon (216GTi five-door), Ian Bone (220 Coupé) and Neil Castle (216GTi three-door), whose cars were photographed for this book.

There is far more to the R8 story than could be accommodated in these pages, but I hope what is here will be enough to satisfy the curious, to whet a few appetites for more, and to encourage some readers to try R8 ownership.